SYMEON CABELL

the
pissed off
writings
of a prophet

Published by Purpose Publishing
1503 Main Street #168 ⚹ Grandview, Missouri
www.purposepublishing.com

ISBN: 978-0-9828379-1-7

Copyright ©2011, Symeon Cabell

Cover design by Sharon Dailey
Editing by Brenda Cotton

Printed in the United States of America

This book, or parts thereof, may not be reproduced, stored in a retrieval system, or transmitted in any form or by means– electronic, mechanical, photocopy, recording, or any other without the prior permission of the publisher.

Inquiries may be addressed to:
www.SymeonCabell.com

This book is available at quantity discounts for bulk purchases. For more information contact,
www.SymeonCabell.com

Scripture used in this book are noted from the KJV of the Bible

Dedication:

To my King. The *only* Life-giver. Reign forever.

Foreword

To God be the glory for such a profound teaching conveyed to readers throughout this book. To present readers with such sound truth, (which has totally been obliterated in most modern day churches) truth that has been derived from the grace God has given author Symeon Cabell, even to remain diligent, obedient, and completely surrendered to Christ. No man could ever present such an insightful message from his own knowledge and ability. What has been revealed in this book has come from the revelation of God. You can clearly see that Symeon presents his message with applied biblical principles and knowledge.

Ahh, speaking of biblical principles and knowledge, we know that God clearly states "my people are destroyed from lack of knowledge" (Hosea 4:6,NIV). He also states in His Word, "To the Jews who had believed him, Jesus said, 'If you hold to my teaching, you are really my disciples. Then you will know the truth, and the truth shall set you free.'" (John 8:31-32, NIV)

Isn't it wonderful to know that we can be free? We do not have to hold to the opinions and teachings of man's own ideology. We can hear the truth and bare witness with the truth knowing that in this truth (biblical truths), we are set free. This is why this book is extremely applicable to the body of Christ, as well as others, because it not only points out the issues that are so prevalent in our culture, Symeon also uses scripture to explain every detail with correct interpretation and uses historical facts to build the foundation of his book.

A dead man is a dead man. A dead man can do nothing. A dead man is totally senseless. We were once spiritually dead and some still are, but by the grace of God, He has given us life. He has awakened us from our dead place and is now radically changing us (and continues to change us) from our corrupt state. We are corrupted because our culture has lost sight of historical and true biblical Christianity.

For all of those who are wholeheartedly after truth, I would highly suggest this book as a tool in helping you to find truth and understanding of what the Gospel really is.

Richard Bowman

Table of Contents:

Introduction i

Chapter 1- Original Intent: Why Man? 1

Chapter 2- Original Intent: Why All This to Begin With? 9

Chapter 3- Predestination: The Christian "F" Word 14

Chapter 4- Faith: That Which Is 27

Chapter 5- Redemption: The Saved "Sinner" 37

Chapter 6- The Fivefold Ministry: Everyone's a Pastor 57

Chapter 7- Hell: A Two Part Saga 75

Chapter 8- The Family: Divine Order 95

Chapter 9- Final Thoughts 121

Biography 128

Introduction

Revival. It has been in my spirit since I was 11 years old. Even then, I could feel that something was coming. I was at a point in my life where I felt that it had been too long... that things had been too idle... there had been too much "nothingness" in the Church. We were busy *telling* people about Jesus, but that was it. We had a great message, too, but without fail, most people would respond with, *"that sounds good, I'll consider it,"* and there were no real results. And what's worse, the same could be said even in our own lives as Christians.

The Gospel was, more or less, just a story we believed to be true and, *"Praise God, Jesus is coming back one day, and we'll be done telling people about Him,"* It was sort of like us telling the world about some good friend we knew that did something pretty spectacular and we just wanted to tell somebody-- basically because He's *your* friend, and it makes *you* look better. (Half of us still don't even want to do that).

As I was discussing this chapter with Rich Bowman, a friend of mine, he made the comparison to politics. He said, "It's like we're Republicans [or whatever], who believe our way is the right way, and if our views are challenged or inquired of by the opposing party, we'll try to voice our position in a politically and culturally correct manner, striving not to draw any sort of offense."

Back to my original thought. When was the last time God had shown up... anywhere? I knew enough of the Bible stories, the accounts, various testimonies, to know He was greater than what I was seeing. That He couldn't be constrained by time or space. That He was omnipresent, and where He is, there is Power... Victory... Glory... Life. Therefore, this and everything that He is, should be everywhere He is manifested.

This feeling became much more of a realization, and revelation, when my mom told me I should look into a particular video sermon. I believe it was called "The X-Blessing" by Bishop Clarence E. McClendon. He spoke of a revelation he received from God, from his reading of the story concerning Jacob blessing Joseph's two sons. Without going into too much detail, it had been missed by many, that Jacob crossed his hands blessing the younger with his right hand and the older with his left forming an "X."
.

The firstborn son was called by commandment to receive the first fruits, the greater and the superior blessing. For he himself was to be dedicated to the LORD as the first fruits a husband and wife's inheritance. However, in this Old Testament account, the younger was given the right hand (hand of favor) blessing over the elder. Jacob, who was called "Israel," being led by the Spirit, blessed the "lesser" – the one put off to the side – with the greater blessing. Not as though Joseph or Jacob thought less of one or the other, for they both were blessed, but it was a matter of election. God decided to give to the one, what man deemed the other was merited… and it formed an "X."

We of this younger generation have been labeled as "Generation X," and though many of us have relished such a title, for various reasons, this "X" is not meant to be a term of endearment, but that which carries negative connotations. One that states we have been "ruled out" and cast off as purposeless, meaningless, and nonchalantly living. Such accusations do not go without some form of merit. Just look at today's world. (I do not feel I need to go in depth with accounts and statistics.) But this brings me to my main point.

Psalm 118:22 records:

The stone which the builders rejected has become the chief cornerstone. (Amplified Bible)

Well that speaks of Christ himself. What does that have to do with this generation, let alone any generation?

God said, "I will use the foolish things to confound the wise." (1 Cor. 1:27) The thing least likely, so that no man may say, "Look at what such a man has done," nor denied that "Truly, God must have been at work." This principle is consistent with everything God is and does, even to the extent of His own Son.

Psalm 22 is the voice of Christ himself, speaking through David, accounting His very anguish and experience on the cross. But there was something that caught my eye a few years back when I was reading through this chapter, all the way at the end. David went on to prophesy:

> ^{30}*A seed* (posterity, a line, a lineage) *shall serve Him; it shall be account to the Lord for* ***a generation***. ^{31}*They shall come, and shall declare His righteousness to a people that shall be born* [*or* yet unborn], *that He has done this.* Psalm 22:30-31 (KJV)

The Amplified Bible says "that it is finished!" God speaks of ***a*** generation that shall accomplish this. Now truly, we are all part of this Last-Day generation, but there is something very peculiar about "my" generation. We don't see fit to hold such vain traditions, thoughtless conditions and stipulations that have encompassed the Church, *His* Church. We have sought a new thing seemingly unwittingly, and it has been leading us, as a body, to radical changes that should have always been, for God is ever-increasing. The problem is that there are so few of us, relatively speaking. The same "whys" we ask, have unfortunately been leading our secular peers, ignorant of the Truth, to ask from their own understanding, "Why Christ?"

Now please don't misunderstand me, as to be putting my generation on a pedestal, even at the expense of diminishing and disrespecting our elders. Those who have continued to "carry their cross" so that we might see there is still one to carry. To be frank, I believe this next generation which has already begun, (I have children of my own) will far surpass, by the grace of God, anything we've ever seen. But all are needed to move in this Last-Day revival as God has desired it to be, showing Himself in indisputable Glory and Truth, such as the world has never seen. In order to do that, though, we must get back to the Truth of the Word, which we have lost, misunderstood, or flat out perverted. Or we will never be able to see, or move in the glory He has prescribe for us in this new and better covenant.

The Pissed off Writings of a Prophet

Chapter 1
Original Intent: Why Man?

Have you ever wondered why, when we preach the Gospel, it so often seems repetitious and mundane; just powerless and uninteresting? Such a far cry from that which we have seen in the New Testament; namely the book of Acts. I truly believe it is not the people we are preaching to that make this "situation" many times, inevitable, but rather the fact that so few us really even understand the Gospel we preach, and I'm *not* just talking about Matthew, Mark, Luke and John. To start to gain an understanding of this powerful Gospel, we have to go back to Genesis [and I'm not talking about the *"your seed will bruise the head of the serpent..."* stuff that every pastor regurgitates].

> [1]*In the beginning God created the heaven and the earth.* [2]*And the earth was without form, and void; and darkness was upon the face of the deep. And the Spirit of God moved upon the face of the waters.* Genesis 1:1-2 (KJV)

Does anyone see a problem with that? Can anybody tell me when God ever created something "void," or if that's even possible?

An accurate description of Satan's kingdom/system and

minion is referred to as *"the one who was, and is not."* (Revelation 17) But God is. He is the Great I AM!

"God created the heaven and the earth...," but we pass up the next space between the period and the following letter "A." We pass it off as Moses proceeding to recount the process of how He did it. The problem is God is not like us, at least not in our fallen state. He doesn't start off with trash, formless voids covered in darkness.

I've heard a few pastors give some insight into this very idea of what happened, but only one really expressed it in a way that identified with my spirit, that was grasped by my mind, and seemed to, at least, *not* contradict the Bible. Where he got it from, I cannot say, except to say God must have just sat him down and told him, much like the account of Creation was given to Moses. This man of God will remain nameless, not because I want to take credit for anything (revelation is from God), but because I don't want to have misrepresented what he was saying. I heard this revelation over a series of messages some years ago but the Spirit has kept some things fresh in my mind all this time.

This man of God (well known to many) stated that God had indeed created the heavens and the earth, with creatures of all sorts, including the angels in heaven. However, sin, or Satan, was "introduced" to a perfect world with no established guardians to protect its physical realms, and thus, the earth became void, and formless, with "darkness" over the face of the deep. A few very interesting points I have acquired over the years support my belief in this revelation. One being Biblical, and the others being scientific observation that we have passed off for so long, not even realizing the implications and probable confirmation of this

Biblical account, as well as the account stated by the man of God.

Scientists have long believed that an asteroid crashed into the earth millions of years ago, laying waste to the former earth and its inhabitants. Now I don't presume to say millions of years ago, or give any extent of time when this may have occurred, nor do I concur with the assessment that what hit the earth was an asteroid. I do, however, wonder where such a notion came from, though. (Some of you may follow where I'm going now.) Luke recorded Jesus' account of what became of Satan when he rebelled against God:

And he said unto them, I beheld Satan as lightning fall from heaven. Luke 10:18 (KJV)

Fall to where?

Isaiah gives us some insight:

[12]How art thou fallen from heaven, O Lucifer, son of the morning! how art thou cut down to the ground, which didst weaken the nations! [13]For thou hast said in thine heart, I will ascend into heaven, I will exalt my throne above the stars of God: I will sit also upon the mount of the congregation, in the sides of the north: [14]I will ascend above the heights of the clouds; I will be like the most High. [15]Yet thou shalt be brought down to hell, to the sides of the pit. [16]They that see thee shall narrowly look upon thee, and consider thee, saying, Is this the man that made the earth to tremble, that did shake kingdoms;

> ^{17}*That made the world as a wilderness, and destroyed the cities thereof; that opened not the house of his prisoners?* Isaiah 14:12-17 (KJV)

We all know of scientists to have some form of high intellectual wherewithal, as much as many of us "people of faith" don't like to admit. But indeed, one must ask the question how such people, with the implications of being secularistic, could come to such a scientific conclusion that so resembles Biblical accounts?

God is God of the heavens and earth, but God is a Spirit. A physical authority had to be installed in the earth in order to see that this couldn't happen again. Thus, God creates man in His image, or very likeness and character. Creatures that would be gods in the flesh establishing God's will and kingdom in the earth, in a godly manner, with godly dominion. Jesus himself recounts what David proclaims in Psalm 82; that we are gods.

> ^{1}*God standeth in the congregation of the mighty; he judgeth among the gods.* (KJV)

This can literally be translated, "*Elohim* standeth in the congregation of *el*."

> ^{2}*How long will ye judge unjustly, and accept the persons of the wicked? Selah.* ^{3}*Defend the poor and fatherless: do justice to the afflicted and needy.* ^{4}*Deliver the poor and needy: rid them out of the hand of the wicked.* ^{5}*They know not, neither will they understand; they walk on in*

darkness: all the foundations of the earth are out of course. ⁶I have said, Ye are gods; and all of you are children of the most High. ⁷But ye shall die like men, and fall like one of the princes (or angels). *⁸Arise, O God, judge the earth: for thou shalt inherit all nations.* (KJV)

I must clear up a major misnomer. Every person that has lived on Earth is not a child of God. John 1:12 says:

But as many as received him (Christ), to them gave he power to become the sons of God, even to them that believe on his name: (KJV)

And Galatians 3:26 reiterates:

For ye are all the children of God by faith in Christ Jesus. (KJV)

When He says all, He is talking directly to *His* children. Consider, Christ actually called a certain group of people "children of the devil." (John 8:44)

I have to point out, concerning this concept of us (the redeemed) being gods, that the Scripture affirms it when God says "ye shall die like men" or as the New Living Translation puts it, "like mere mortals." Which implies, we must be more that men.

Well, I just don't get how, or… how?

Consider that God breathed the Breath of Life into Adam. Now we know that this Life is much more that just physical living. So much more, that we may presume to say it's not even talking about physical life. If so, why was Adam still breathing when he ate of the fruit from the tree of knowledge of good and evil? God told him face to face, if he ever did, he would *surely* die.

This takes me to the most revolutionary sermon I have ever heard, and, quite possibly, will ever hear; because it set the foundation of Truth that has lead me to so many lost discoveries in the Word. It was given by the man of God, Isaac Pitre during Dominion Camp Meeting at World Harvest Church, headed by a man I literally hold in the highest regard (as far as men are concerned), Pastor Rod Parsley.

The funny thing is, his message came from John 3:16. Pitre pointed out that the Church has missed it. He said, it wasn't that we got it *all* wrong; we just didn't have it all right.

Everyone knows John 3:16. We quote it every time we witness to an unbeliever. The problem is, we don't fully understand it.

> *For God so loved the world, that He gave His only begotten Son, that whosoever believeth on him, should not perish, but shall have everlasting life.*

"Well what's so hard to understand about that? It seems pretty self explanatory."

You're right... if you know what the words mean.

Perish:

Apollymi (Greek)-

To be destroyed due to separation, to be cut off, rendered useless

Have:

(English)-

To possess, own

Everlasting:

Aiōnios (Greek)-

Without beginning and end, that which always has been and always will be.

Such stipulations cannot be given to a man who has a beginning, implying (self evidently I believe) that this is an adjective referring to **quality** rather than **quantity**. How can one measure something with no beginning or end?

Life:

Zōē (Greek)-

Of the absolute fullness of life, both essential and ethical, which belongs to God, and through him both to the hypostatic "logos" and to Christ in whom the "logos" put on human nature.

Quite simply, it's "the God kind of life."

With this understanding, the Scripture can literally be translated:

> For God so loved the world, that He gave His only begotten Son, that whosoever believeth on him, should **no longer be cut off and rendered useless, but shall possess (presently) the quality of Life God Himself has**.

We now see that this Scripture is not about heaven, or our "eternal" life when we get to heaven. This Scripture is talking about the separation from the Life of God, that was caused by sin, the death, or severance, of our Life-source connection, and the way we got it back. But that's for another chapter.

Man was perfect, just like God. His very reflection. Isaac Pitre said it like this, "We had flowing in us, what God has flowing in Him." The very Spirit of God. The Breath of Life, which kept us in continual (everlasting) communion with God, in order that He might establish parallel kingdoms. Spirit ruling the spiritual realms, and spirit in the flesh, or in the physical, ruling the physical realms. But all of one mind; His mind.

Chapter 2
Original Intent:
Why *All* This To Begin With?

It's a question that men from all walks of life have asked in some form or another. Why are we, and all of this, here? I believe the problem is that Christians seem to be the least to actively ask that question.

"God created us for a purpose. We have value to Him. He loves us."

One problem; what happened before all that? Why did He create anything? Forget the part about giving us purpose, or what purpose we each have. Why us and the universe in general? I believe this is even more pertinent for a Christian to grasp than those who don't know the Truth because it sets the foundation and "motive" [if you will] for understanding why God has, is, and will have done anything. For all eternity. Praise Him! Proverbs 9:10 declares the key to such revelation. Follow me.

The fear of the LORD is the beginning of wisdom, and knowledge of the Holy One is understanding. (NIV)

There are a few things we must point out before we begin. The <u>fear</u> of the LORD cannot *completely* be equated to the "fear" we normally speak of, nor can it be simply passed off to be something different than what it says.

The word "fear," used here is the Hebrew word "*yir'ah.*" It means just that, "fear," but with the connotation of reverence; that which is dreadful and exceeding.

Well, let's look at the Scripture as a whole. The word "and" is tying two parts together. Notice I said tying, not to be mistaken with equaling. God is very particular about words. With words, He framed and formed the universe. He says what He means to say and will not repeat Himself needlessly. He is correlating the "fear of the LORD" with "knowledge of the Holy One, and "the beginning of wisdom" with "understanding." This starts to give us a better picture of terminology.

Well how does knowledge correlate to fear? It is said, "we fear what we do not understand, what we can't 'see'; what we do not know." Unfortunately there is some truth to that, but that's a whole different message and is to some degree quite opposite of what is being conveyed.

If we have knowledge of God (if we **know** God), it is a revelatory knowledge that not only give us "understanding," or logistics and facts about God, but rather constitutes revelation that unites us as one with the Most High God and we begin to see Him as He is. Unfathomable, dreadful, fantastical, beyond comprehension, all powerful, all knowing, ever-present, etc. (the list goes on…). With this, we begin to "see" or "know" this exceeding reverence for such a "Being," and one that will most certainly invoke fear, but a godly fear. Jesus himself says, *"Fear not the one who is able to destroy the body, but Him who is able to destroy both the body and the soul."* (Matt. 10:28) No one is capable of such things, save God. Consider this word, "knowledge," is based in the same word, "knew," that the King James Bible uses to convey intimacy between a man and a woman, or the "two becoming one flesh."

"Well what does this have to do with why God created everything, or anything?"

Keep following me. To shed some light on this question, we actually have to go back a chapter. (Leave it to God to do that.) Proverbs 8:22-31 give a self-accounting of wisdom:

> [22]*The LORD brought me forth as the first of his works, before his deeds of old;* [23]*I was appointed from eternity, from the beginning, before the world began.* [24]*When there were no oceans, I was given birth, when there were no springs abounding with water;* [25]*before the mountains were settled in place, before the hills, I was given birth,* [26]*before he made the earth or its fields or any of the dust of the world.* [27]*I was there when he set the heavens in place, when he marked out the horizon on the face of the deep,* [28]*when he established the clouds above and fixed securely the fountains of the deep,* [29]*when he gave the sea its boundary so the waters would not overstep his command, and when he marked out the foundations of the earth.* [30]*Then I was the craftsman at his side. I was filled with delight day after day, rejoicing always in his presence,* [31]*rejoicing in his whole world and delighting in*

mankind. (NIV)

I want you to consider something. It says that wisdom was brought forth as the first of His works, and/but goes on to say that it was appointed from eternity. Hold on to that. I need to point out a few more things. It was there from the beginning, but before the world began, before the world was created. Before time, "*In* the beginning." Time had no purpose or place for an eternal God before the physical realm and its limits were manifested. I need to note one more thing that is very critical to grasp. Wisdom was not only present before and during the awesome wonders of God's creative activity, but was the very craftsman at His side. That means from wisdom stemmed the power to create the heavens and the earth, as well as the very design.

I need you to understand something because I'm 'bout to get to the point.

God is bound by His word.

"Duh, everybody (Christian-speaking) knows that."

You are not following; He is bound to the same "process" we *assume* He was just giving to us. In order for wisdom to come about, the Scripture says the fear of the LORD has to have been present; it is the beginning of wisdom.

"So what are you saying, God feared Himself...?"

Exactly!

This is why we had to lay such ground work about what the fear of the LORD is. In eternity past, God "took inquiry" of Himself, considered Himself, knew Himself, feared Himself. He concluded that He is Jehovah God, the Great I Am, the Everlasting Father, the One Who is Worthy of All.

Mind you, this process was not exactly an event that

happened at some point in time. God is eternal; He is everlasting; His very thoughts have no beginning, nor end. The Scripture itself testifies that wisdom was appointed from eternity. And with such knowledge, wisdom burst forth executing a plan. A plan of creation, and in such, a creation that would glorify Him to the fullest, and "eternal" extent. Who, or what, could or would be worthy of such a task... but Himself. So He fashioned creatures like unto Himself, filled with Himself, that could reproduce more "him's", and as Isaac Pitre stated in his sermon mentioned in Chapter 1, God said, *"If he is truly like Me, than he's gon' want to rule and reign like Me. He's gon' wanna dominate like Me."* Thus:

> *Let them have dominion over the fish of the sea, and over the fowl of the air, and over the cattle, and over all the earth, and over every creeping thing that creepeth upon the earth.* Genesis 1:26b (KJV)

"Quick question, why everything else? There's a whole universe out there."

Simple thoughts for your consideration. When man was created he was in the physical, but not limited to the physical. Man is a spirit-being, just like Daddy. Consider he had the power to move in and out of the physical realm just as all other spirit beings.

"Well, what are you trying to say?"

Our spirits were connected as one to the eternal Spirit. What would you do if you could move at a rate that makes the speed of light look like it's standing still? Anybody find it interesting that scientists believe they've found evidence of fossils of bacteria on Mars?

Chapter 3
Predestination: The Christian "F" Word

It's funny. For a word that is mentioned four times in the New Testament, we Christians sure have an interesting way of dismissing or avoiding the concept. Yet, we claim to be proclaiming the Truth of the Gospel. The word "elect(ed)" or "election" is mentioned, at least in this context, over 20 times throughout the Bible.

I first of all want to take a look at a thing called logic.

Elect(ion)-

To chose or appoint an individual or group for any particular reason(s).

I want you to note that anytime an official is elected, they do not place themselves into the office, they are chosen by the powers that be.

Predestine, or predestination-

Derived from:

1. Pre - before

2. Destiny, or destination- Outcome, event, and/or location that

has been planned out, to reach or achieve.

Put them together and you get an outcome, event, and/or location that has already been planned out, to reach or achieve.

"Well Sym those are just your definitions."

True to some degree. But that's just fine. Let's just go back into the "Amazing Concordance of Strong."

Elect(ion)

Bachiyr (Hebrew)-

Select, chose, elect

    From *bachar*- to choose, to appoint, to require

Eklektos (Greek)-

Select, chose, elect

    From *ek*- out of

    And *lego*- to 'lay' forth, or to name or call out

    So, biblically termed, one can define election as being selected and appointed out of; by name, you were called, and that being a requirement.

    That's a whole 3 books in itself. But the most intriguing thing happens when I looked up the Greek word used in the Bible for "predestinate."

Predestinate

Proorizō (Greek)-

To limit in advance, predetermine, ordain

From *pro*- in front of, prior to, before, ever

And *horizō*- to mark out or bound, to decree, to specify, declare, determine

--Funny enough, horizō comes from the word, *"horion,"* or boundary-line

"Sym, what does this have to do with anything you've put in this book thus far. It seems like you're just trying to force something here."

You may remember that I said in eternity past God considered Himself, though it was no absolute point in time or space, but eternally came to a plan. A plan that would glorify Him to the fullest.

"Yeah, you said man, made like unto Him, would give Him the highest praise."

True, but there's only one problem. How can you fully appreciate something you don't fully understand, or never even had the chance to experience?

"I'm not following."

Let me put it another way. Without seeing His wrath, how

could you ever perceive the depths of His mercy? Without seeing His hatred for sin, how could you ever experience such unconditional love. God is so many things that we never would have had an exhaustive need to know or experience, had we never fallen.

"Wait, tell me you're not implying that God made and continues to make us sin."

Not at all. I'm saying God in His wisdom had a plan that would reveal Himself in His fullness to His greatest creation.

"So like I said, you're trying to say God made all this happen; He wanted it."

Consider this. Who is the author of sin?

"Satan."

Why did he fall?

"Because he became conceited, greedy and selfish, wanting God's throne to himself."

"AAANNNNNNNNNNNNT! Wrong answer, Bob."

Jesus said he (Satan) was a murderer from the beginning. (John 8:44) Can anybody explain this? How about the fact that Christ is called the Lamb slain *before* the foundations of the world? (Rev. 13:8) Here's another issue. Man was perfect; spirit, body and soul. How does he manage to sin?

"Well, see he had a choice."

Ok, well if that's the case, what's to stop us from sinning in heaven?

"I don't know, but there it is. You're saying that this is all on God. That God makes us sin, that God wants people to go to hell, that Satan was just a pawn in some sick game. Well, explain to me this? If this is the case, that God controls all our destinies and what we do, good or bad, why should I, or anybody else, be punished for what He planned for us to do?"

Good question and on that note…

^{1}I speak the truth in Christ—I am not lying, my conscience confirms it in the Holy Spirit— ^{2}I have great sorrow and unceasing anguish in my heart. ^{3}For I could wish that I myself were cursed and cut off from Christ for the sake of my brothers, those of my own race, ^{4}the people of Israel. Theirs is the adoption as sons; theirs the divine glory, the covenants, the receiving of the law, the temple worship and the promises. ^{5}Theirs are the patriarchs, and from them is traced the human ancestry of Christ, who is God over all, forever praised! Amen.

⁶It is not as though God's word had failed. For not all who are descended from Israel are Israel. ⁷Nor because they are his descendants are they all Abraham's children. On the contrary, "It is through Isaac that your offspring will be reckoned." ⁸In other words, it is not the natural children who are God's children, but it is the children of the promise who are regarded as Abraham's offspring. ⁹For this was how the promise was stated: "At the appointed time I will return, and Sarah will have a son."

¹⁰Not only that, but Rebekah's children had one and the same father, our father Isaac. ¹¹Yet, before the twins were born or had done anything good or bad—in order that God's purpose in election might stand: ¹²not by works but by him who calls—she was told, "The older will serve the younger." ¹³Just as it is written: "Jacob I loved, but Esau I hated."

¹⁴What then shall we say? Is God unjust? Not at all! ¹⁵For he says to Moses, "I will have mercy on whom I have mercy, and I will have compassion on whom I have compassion." ¹⁶It does not, therefore, depend on man's desire or effort, but on God's mercy. ¹⁷For the Scripture says to Pharaoh: "I raised you up for this very purpose, that I might display my power in you and that my name might be proclaimed in all the earth." ¹⁸Therefore God has mercy on whom he wants to have mercy, and he hardens whom he wants to harden.

¹⁹One of you will say to me: "Then why does God still blame us? For who resists his will?" ²⁰But who are you, O man, to talk back to God? "Shall what is formed say to him who formed it, 'Why did you make me like this?'" ²¹Does not the potter have the right to make out of the same lump of clay some pottery for noble purposes

and some for common use?

[22] What if God, choosing to show his wrath and make his power known, bore with great patience the objects of his wrath—prepared for destruction? [23] What if he did this to make the riches of his glory known to the objects of his mercy, whom he prepared in advance for glory— [24] even us, whom he also called, not only from the Jews but also from the Gentiles? Romans 9:1-24 (NIV)

Let me make this clear and bold. **Our God is SOVEREIGN**. No "and's," "if's," or "but's" about it. He is in full control of everything. Jesus said, *"All authority in heaven and earth is given to Me."* (Matt. 28:18) He says He gives mercy to those He wants and those "prepared for destruction" are purposed, and borne "with great patience," in order that He might show those of us He *has* called "the riches of His glory [and mercy]."

"Why would He do something like that? I thought the Bible says that He desires that none should perish."

It most assuredly does. But let me see if I can give you some understanding on these matters.

First off, consider God has what He desires, and what He **would** [as I refer to it], as in what He would have, or what He would do. Some will refer to this as His perfect will vs. his permissive will. But God has one will. His good, acceptable and perfect will. (Rom. 12:2) There are things God desires that will never come to pass because He had something greater of purpose in mind, but He has still made many things in His heart known to us that we might grow in wisdom and love towards

Him. Our Father loves us and sent his Son to die not only for the sins of the elect but for those He knew would reject Him anyways. Even so, consider, God desires that men not sin against Him, yet that continues to go on *and* increase in measure.

Let me give you an analogy that God has been building in my mind to put some practicality and logic to this.

Scenario 1:

A man has a limitless amount of money and says to a large crowd that does not know him, "If any of you want a million dollars, I'll give it to you. Just come and get it." Some would immediately run to the man. Some would possibly make their way slowly towards him checking to see what others are doing. Still many would dismiss it entirely, as skepticism comes in. Some may even stand around not making a choice at all, but just watching.

Scenario 2:

A man has a limitless amount of money and says to a large crowd that does not know him, "I have set aside a million dollars apiece for each man (or woman) but I will only choose 10 of you. No doubt, people would try to get his attention with various types of "works" and actions, but he is not choosing based off what he sees.

Consider, in which situation will the people who received be more grateful? Let's go further.

The man returns, and asks those whom he has given this gift, to do various tasks for him. As you might imagine, in scenario one, some would follow instruction due to gratitude, but others most likely would put up some type of dispute due to resentment, or at least hesitation, because "they didn't know there would be any strings attached."

But those in scenario two, I would imagine, would show us a completely different story. "Just name it!"

Now consider those of us who have been called from the beginning, before we had yet entered this Earth. Chosen, not because we had something special or great about us, at least in and of ourselves, that set us apart from anyone else, but because, God simply said, "I want you. Not him." We could have been one of the ones He didn't choose.

"I don't understand. Joshua said "Choose ye this day whom ye will serve..." (Joshua 24:15)

It's funny because Jesus almost seems to respond with a rebuttal to that very statement, *"You didn't choose me, I chose you."* (John 15:16)

"It seems like it would be a contradiction, though."

Not at all. You must consider that the Bible (or the "Scriptures") wasn't always present. Nor did they always have millennia and innumerable generations to pass down precepts. If all you knew was that God chooses, what would move your faith into action? God had to give a commandment to act, but came back with an empowering and informative statement that sets the truth of the matter in order. So many of us will see one thing in the Bible that supports *our* personal theology, and as we come across something else, we will just disregard or pervert it to fit our theology, because otherwise, that would be a "contradiction."

"Well then what do I do? Who do I witness to? Why witness?"

First and foremost, do as you were commanded. *"Go ye into all the world and preach the gospel to every creature."* (Mark 15:16) As well, you don't know who God has chosen, but you do know He died for the world so that makes everyone a "potential candidate."

There's always the "silly," but nonetheless very serious question that may come from this, "How do I know that I am one of the chosen?" John said *"these things I write to you that believe in the name of the Son of God that you may **know** you have eternal life."* (1 John 5:13) The Holy Spirit bears witness with your spirit that you are sealed by the Spirit of God. (Romans 8:16; Eph. 1:13-14)

Some Scriptures for consideration:

[10]*Then the disciples came and said to him, "Why do you speak to them in parables?"*
[11]*And he answered them, "To you it has been given to

know the secrets of the kingdom of heaven, but to them it has not been given. Matt. 13:10-11

^{12}But as many as received him, to them gave he power to become the sons of God, even to them that believe on his name: ^{13}Which were born, not of blood, nor of the will of the flesh, nor of the will of man, but of God. John 1:12-13

^{39}Therefore they could not believe. For again Isaiah said,^{40}"He has blinded their eyes and hardened their heart, lest they see with their eyes, and understand with their heart, and turn, and I would heal them." ^{41}Isaiah said these things because he saw his glory and spoke of him. John 12:39-41

^{6}"I have revealed you to those whom you gave me out of the world. They were yours; you gave them to me and they have obeyed your word. ^{9}I pray for them. I am not praying for the world, but for those you have given me, for they are yours. ^{12}While I was with them, I protected them and kept them safe by that name you gave me. None has been lost except the one doomed to destruction so that Scripture would be fulfilled." John 17:6,9,12

And when the Gentiles heard this, they began rejoicing and glorifying the word of the Lord, and as many as were appointed to eternal life believed. Acts 13:48

Who hath saved us, and called us with an holy calling, not according to our works, but according to his own purpose and grace, which was given us in Christ Jesus before the world began

2 Tim 1:9

⁴According as he hath chosen us in him before the foundation of the world, that we should be holy and without blame before him in love: ⁵Having predestinated us unto the adoption of children by Jesus Christ to himself, according to the good pleasure of his will,

¹¹ In whom also we have obtained an inheritance, being predestinated according to the purpose of him who worketh all things after the counsel of his own will: Eph 1:4-5,11

The Pissed off Writings of a Prophet

Chapter 4:
Faith: That Which Is

I hardly know where to begin. It *seems* He gives us enough grace, to have enough faith, that somehow we [merely] exist as Christians. There is such a lack of understanding out there. And people don't seem to get that this is what faith is, knowledge.

Let me give you my definition (very simplified). Faith is "perceived *revelation* knowledge that is believed producing manifestations." You must understand how "broadly" I use the term manifestation.

Now let's start from the beginning. *"Faith is the substance of things hoped for, the evidence . . .".*

I'm playin'. But truly from such a verse (which we'll get back to later), we understand that faith is not based off of what we "see."

"Oh, well I know that."

No you don't. If you did then, you'd understand that if you can "see" it, faith can't be involved in that particular realm, whatever "it" may be. I'll explain that later too.

Two verses sum up for me what faith is. If I knew nothing else about it, these could probably do it.

    1) *Faith come by hearing, and hearing by the word of God.* (Romans 10:17)

    2) *The just shall live by faith.* (Habakkuk 2:4; Galatians 3:11)

Two verses. Now we have to do some *"extrapolation and mathimaticaltations and summaries of the summational sums."* I'm playin', but let's dissect these two verses.

Where does faith come from?

"Hearing."

Hearing what?

"The word of God."

Whoa! Back up. It says hearing <u>by</u> the word of God. Meaning that as faith comes by hearing, hearing comes about by the process [and workings] of... the word of God, even in term of "hearing" being an ability empowered by such. This may not be making sense to you, or you may think it's old news, or too obvious, so let go deeper.

The process of the word of God:

In Matthew 16, Jesus asked His disciples, *"Who do men say that I am?"* They gave various answers. He then asked them, *"Who do you say that I am?"* Peter spoke up and said, *"Thou art the Christ. The Son of the Living God."* (If that don't stir up the Spirit in you...) How is it that Peter came to such a conclusion when no one else was saying anything like it? None of Jesus' other disciples would even speak up.

He (Jesus) very well could have been "just" a prophet, as the disciple had reported to his initial question. We go on to find that Christ revealed such an answer. *"Blessed are you Simon bar Jonah (Peter), for flesh and blood has not reveal this to you but my Father who is in heaven."* This tells us that no mere man could've told Peter such a thing, including Peter himself, being that he was flesh and blood. He "heard," or was given the answer from an "unseen" God (for God is Invisible). But the *presence* of the Word of God (Christ), who was unknown and "unseen" to the world, ignited a truth in Peter that sprang forth an action of worship and declaration, not only that Jesus was the Christ but that now a covenant had been struck between the Father and His new heir and son, Peter.

So what's the point of this? One, man cannot in and of himself discern any truth of God.

"How can you say that?"

Jesus said, *"I am the Way, the <u>Truth</u>, and the Life."* (John

14:6) And according to Christ you can't know him unless the Father reveals him to you.

So, point two, when we encounter the word -- and we know the Bible to be the physical manifestation of God's Wisdom to us -- it begins to revolutionize and transform our lives. We become enabled to "hear" what the Spirit is saying. That's why Christ would always implore when He spoke a mystery, *"Who hath ears to hear, let him hear."*

So, a primary source of our faith comes from hearing, or **perceiving** the *revealed* revelation of God through His word. Putting it simply: read the Bible, gather faith (perceived revelation knowledge that is believed producing manifestations).

"Well I knew that."

Then why don't you believe what you read?

"What are you talking about?"

We've already started getting into what the Bible actually says as opposed to what we make it to say, but we'll continue further in coming chapters.

"Well what about the second verse you said you'd talk about."

The just live by faith, and faith comes from perceiving

what the Word says about us. (How else can I put this without getting all philosophical?) What the Bible says about you is the truth about you. (You see so many of these great things, and fail to understand they were put there simply to tell you about you. But we can't see it, nor would we believe it, because we're still looking at what we can 'see.')

> *Now faith is the substance of things hoped for, the evidence of things not seen.* Hebrews 11:1 (KJV)

Faith is the substance, the "material" constituting what that thing is made of that you are presently waiting for. The Bible says hope that is seen is not hope at all. (Rom. 8:24) So that which you have prayed and believed for actually consists of your faith until the creative action manifests.

Let's go on to the second part of the verse, *"the evidence of things not seen."* Let me first say before this, that the Bible says without faith it's impossible to please Him (God). (Hebrews 11:6) So faith is the foundational proof (knowledge; perceived, and in turn, believed) that assures us what we don't "see" is really there. Evidence is conclusive proof that either something is or has already happened. It points to that which is, like a sign. God provides proof, tangible or intangible, that the invisible, past, present or to come, "IS", and the only way to please Him is to know what you can't "see." Notice that "substance" and "evidence" are 'concrete' words. Concrete in the fact that they are... there.

Let me try to explain because I'm most likely not making sense to you, or I sound kind of pointless. If there is substance, where that substance is, emptiness is not. Where evidence is, reality is, fact is. The Bible says that faith is a substance and is evidence. Faith must be a good thing, to be pleasing to God, and to be such a requirement (without faith it is impossible to please Him). So if it's good, it's complete. Therefore faith, in and of itself, has nothing to do with degrees of belief and/or doubt, nor is there any sort of place for doubt concerning it.

Then came the disciples to Jesus apart, and said, Why could not we cast him out? And Jesus said unto them, Because of your unbelief: for verily I say unto you, If ye have faith as a grain of mustard seed, ye shall say unto this mountain, Remove hence to yonder place; and it shall remove; and nothing shall be impossible unto you. Matthew 17:19-20 (KJV)

The comparison of faith to a mustard seed infers quite clearly that faith is not regarded in quantity but rather its quality. See, the mustard seed is one of the smallest seeds in the plant kingdom but grows to be one of the largest herbal trees on Earth. From a couple millimeters in diameter to 12 feet tall. It's potent. When Peter walked on water, he responded by faith; his certainty in the truth of Jesus' word to him, *"Come."* Interestingly enough, Jesus later reveals that when he (Peter) did this, he accomplished it with "little faith." Apparently the quantity was irrelevant. It wasn't until what he knew shifted to what he was seeing around him. Immediately he sank. Doubt and faith don't mix. So what Jesus is saying is, "If your faith be complete and full, like this potent mustard seed, regardless of how small a thing it may seem, you will reap an exponentially multiplied harvest. If you only know a little about Me, if that which you know is the Truth, I AM eternal and infinite and you will, and can only, reap such a harvest." If you've seen part of God, you've seen all of God (if you can follow me). I'm not making a claim that we can even begin to fathom the fullness of the Great I Am. My point is that God is. He is not composed of parts but rather is All in all, from beginning to end, He Is the same.

This is faith. Knowing the truth about God. It is *not* making up something to make us feel better about trials and tribulations when they come our way. We say, "That's not God trying to teach you something. He's not like that. That's just the devil." But we'll read over the very Scripture stating that Christ himself learned obedience through suffering. (Hebrews 5:8) And we go one way or the other, not considering that both may be true. God *is* trying to teach you [and that lesson may be for others as well] showing Himself strong in you, while using that which the devil would desire to destroy you with. But rest assured that God is fully in control of the "rain" that pours on the just and the unjust. (Matthew 5:45)

Let me give you something practical. I'm conceptualizing faith as well as the make-up of many people's "faith," but I'd venture to guess it's hard to understand unless I give some kind of example.

I recall two Scriptures, or a least a singular Scripture and a set, that no one likes to mention or talk about, *yet everyone still seems to have a "full gospel church."* (We barely want to talk about Job.)

Is it not from the mouth of the Most High that both calamities and good things come? Lamentations 3:38

I put the NIV translation out there just to ease you into it. The King James Version actually says:

> *Out of the mouth of the Most High proceedeth not evil and good?*

¡Interesante! (Spanish for "Interesting") Let's go to 1 Kings 22:

Verse 8-9:

> [8] *And the king of Israel (Ahab) said unto Jehoshaphat, There is yet one man, Micaiah the son of Imlah, by whom we may enquire of the LORD: but I hate him; for he doth not prophesy good concerning me, but evil. And Jehoshaphat said, Let not the king say so (You shouldn't say that).* [9] *Then the king of Israel called an officer, and said, Hasten hither Micaiah the son of Imlah.*

Verse 15-23:

> [15] *So he came to the king (Jehoshaphat). And the king said unto him, Micaiah, shall we go against Ramothgilead to battle, or shall we forbear? And he answered him, Go, and prosper: for the LORD shall deliver it into the hand of the king.* [16] *And the king said unto him, How many times shall I adjure thee that thou tell me nothing but that which is true in the name of the LORD?* [17] *And he (Micaiah) said, I saw all Israel scattered upon the hills, as sheep that have not a shepherd: and the LORD said, These have no master: let them return every man to his house in peace.* [18] *And the king of Israel said*

unto Jehoshaphat, Did I not tell thee that he would prophesy no good concerning me, but evil? [19] And he (Micaiah) said, Hear thou therefore the word of the LORD: I saw the LORD sitting on his throne, and all the host of heaven standing by him on his right hand and on his left. [20] And the LORD said, Who shall persuade Ahab, that he may go up and fall at Ramothgilead? And one said on this manner, and another said on that manner. [21] And there came forth a spirit, and stood before the LORD, and said, I will persuade him. [22] And the LORD said unto him, Wherewith (How will you do this)? And he said, I will go forth, and I will be a lying spirit in the mouth of all his prophets. And he (the LORD) said, Thou shalt persuade him, and prevail also: go forth, and do so. [23] Now therefore, behold, the LORD hath put a lying spirit in the mouth of all these thy prophets, and the LORD hath spoken evil concerning thee.

Can this be? The God of Truth would intentionally send deception in order to accomplish that which He proposed? We have to get outside our own comfort zones. We put God in a "box" that fits our understanding and push Him one way or another... or another.

"If I believe that everything bad that happens is Satan and Satan alone, then at least I have hope that I can rebuke and rebuke. But if it's God in control of this matter... who can stand against Him? Where is my hope? How can I opposed the Almighty?"

How, indeed! But your problem is that you try to reason and fit God into your theology, rather than receiving by that which is invisible, that God, regardless of what the situation may look like, will always be God. And He causes all things to work together for the **good** of them that love Him and are called... *called*, according to *His* purpose. (Rom. 8:28) He will be glorified and will go about it in a manner that can only be <u>righteous</u>, regardless of how we view the situation.

Faith is not about a "feeling," or what we'd like to believe, or what makes us feel better about a situation, nor can it be <u>based</u> off our "experiences" in life. Faith is the perceived and believed revelation knowledge of the Truth, that which Is.

Chapter 5
Redemption: The Saved "Sinner"

It's a term you've probably not heard before, but sums up the theology of 99% of Christians I've encountered in my life whether in person, on TV, or by account of another. It's quite a shame because God had something so much better in mind when He sent His only Son.

See, the Bible's reason for Christ coming goes much further than this mundane concept many have of "saving us from our sins." I'm not saying that being saved from sin is a mundane concept but I'm speaking rather to the understanding of that concept which people have. The Bible says that *"for this purpose was the Son of God manifested, that He might destroy (raze) the works of the devil."* (1 John 3:8)

Raze:

To tear down, demolish, annihilate, destroy completely, (especially by fire), overturn, dismantle.

I have heard a literal translation of the word to mean: *To cause to cease to be, as though it never existed.*

Christ came to remove any semblance of the Enemy's

devices. The Bible says we've been translated from the kingdom of darkness to the kingdom of Light. (Colossians 1:13) Yes, he came to save us from our sins, but that could only be accomplished by removing the power of the source.

When we sinned, and by we, I mean Adam (thanks, Adam!), man was cut off from his source of Power, his source of Life. Therefore, man didn't exactly "hand over" his authority to Satan, as we normally perceive it, but rather the authority to rule here went to the highest bidder, the most powerful one present, Satan. That's why he's called, *"the god of this world."* (2 Corin. 4:4) Not as in the actual earth, but the system of sin that had been established when sin perverted a "good" world. But not only did we "give up" authority, as I've said, we were cut off. We existed as the living-dead. Our bodies were no longer controlled by our spirits in connection with His Spirit; our spirits were dead and dormant inside. We existed as purely natural creatures controlled by natural actions and instincts, perverted by evil. We were called *"slaves to sin"* (Romans 6:20) because we had no ability to pursue spiritual and righteous endeavors. We were essentially always "at the whim of a mad man" who had power to sway and influence our very souls. You must remember man is a spirit, so our body and soul were created to be controlled by such. And Satan is the great counterfeit, so what would his obvious action be? Replace the Spirit of God in us.

So what did Christ actually do?

He destroyed the works of the Enemy stripping him of any power or authority he had.

Yes, we all [generally] seem to know that; the Enemy is a defeated foe. But we have so little understanding about what Christ, by doing that, did for us.

Romans 6:1-11

What shall we say, then? Shall we go on sinning so that grace may increase? ²By no means! <u>We died to sin; how can we live in it any longer?</u> ³Or don't you know that all of us who were baptized into Christ Jesus <u>were baptized into his death</u>? ⁴We were therefore buried with him through baptism into death in order that, just as Christ was raised from the dead through the glory of the Father, we too may live a new life.

*⁵If we have been united with him like this in his death, we will certainly also be united with him in his resurrection. ⁶For we know that our old self was crucified with him **so that the body of sin might be done away with**, that we should no longer be slaves to sin— ⁷because **anyone who has died has been freed from sin**. ⁸<u>Now if we died with Christ, we believe that we will also live with him</u>. ⁹For we know that since Christ was raised from the dead, <u>he cannot die again</u>; death no longer has mastery over him. ¹⁰<u>The death he died, he died to sin **once for all**</u>; but the life he lives, he lives to God. ¹¹<u>In the same way</u>, count yourselves **dead to sin but alive to God <u>in Christ Jesus</u>**.*

Well what's that all speaking of? All the bold characters and underlining. What's that all about?

I can't tell you how many Christian I hear declare

the truth that Satan is defeated, but continue to go on in the manifestation of sin claiming it has something to do with our flesh, or, in other words, the sinful nature stemming from these bodies of evil and temptation. Well then I must ask, when the Bible speaks of the flesh, or the sinful nature, what is it referring to? Is this actually the corrupted physical body, **or** is it the nature: the habits and desires of this natural existence? The Bible actually speaks on behalf of both circumstances.

Romans 6, along with so many other Scriptures, testifies to the circumstance of sinful nature in the flesh. We are accounted as being crucified with Christ doing away with this "body of sin," this "slavery" to sinful nature or desire. Our deeds are no more dictated by sin. We know that *"He who knew no sin became sin for us,"* (2 Corin. 5:21) and this crucifixion we partook in resulted in death. A death *"he died to sin <u>once for all</u>."* The Scriptures say that the death he died [once for all] is the very death we died. He's not dying again… and again and again and again. Therefore, neither do we. This body of sin, this sinful nature is gone. The old self is dead. Dead men cannot act. They're dead. We are alive to God *in* Christ. Our resurrection was through Christ to a new man. So if the resurrection itself is through Christ then, our very life and nature is through Christ. Otherwise, we have no life, because what we were before is dead; therefore, there's nothing left to sustain us. No character. Nothing driving life. No soul. Nothing outside of him.

Hold on. Doesn't the Bible speak of mortifying the flesh and dying daily (Romans 8:13; 1 Corin. 15:31), as in… *"and again and again and again."*

Very good, we can never discount Scripture for

theology sake. The point I'm making above is that sinful nature/desire is no more a part of you. It does not stem from you. It is not of you. You are not bound to it, because it is done away with in you. The problem is that Satan is still a liar and we *do* still live in physical bodies. Follow me closely.

Natural desire is fine in a righteous context. Men and women have a natural sexual desire for one another. This is God-given and had to be so, otherwise the human race would have stopped at Adam and Eve. The problem is when you act on it outside of its godly environment, and as many know, action is not just an outward manifestation. The Enemy would have you believe that your flesh is subjected to wickedness (a perversion of godly natural affections) which is a lie, and then have you believe that this seemingly "natural" desire will not be quelled until it is satisfied. This is when you put that wicked thing away and died to a fleshly desire. Paul goes as far as saying that he beats (not to be taken as literal mutilation) his body in subjection to his own will and true nature, godliness. This is our example and model. We walk not by sight, nor after the flesh (merely natural means) but by the Spirit. Just because you feel something doesn't mean it's your own, nor did it have to originate in you. So now, *"we die to sin."* (1 Peter 2:24)

As I mentioned, the Bible also speaks to the very concept of our physical body as a result of salvation. Press on further from Romans 6 to chapter 8, and verse 11:

> *But if the Spirit of him that raised up Jesus from the dead dwell in you, he that raised up Christ from the dead shall also quicken your mortal bodies by his Spirit that dwelleth in you.* (KJV)

The word "quicken" means to make alive, or give life to. The implication, as the Spirit gave life (and the Spirit can only give one kind of Life) to the dead body of Christ, so will he give life to our *mortal* bodies. AKA, physical body.

So, if I hear another person give that wicked, completely un-Biblical line "We're human…" I am going to… pray for them. Gotta be godly. The phrase "we're human" or "we're only human" refers to the nature of carnality. These words are completely true when referring to a man with no covenant (non-believer). He, or she, is quite truthfully "only human." But the Bible tells me I'm much, much more. The Life-force of God is now my very life-force, not merely some kind of addition. That "human" nature; that lacking, flawed nature has died. We call him the "old man." "Old" as in "former." The nature I used to have. But now because my faith ensures Christ is not only living in me, but through me, my new and actual nature, the thing that is natural to me is godliness.

Well, what about Romans 7? Huh? What do you have to say about that?

Believe it or not I actually already explained that. I'll be writing forever if I have to give explanation for everything people could read, but I will say this quickly concerning your reference to what Paul was saying in chapter 7. Consider the very next chapter and more specifically, the first couple verses of the chapter (Romans 8). "*…hath made me free from the law of sin and death.*"

Though many things I just addressed before, speak

concerning the area of the soul and mind of a man, we should probably touch on this much more directly and holistically, because as Jeremiah said, *"the heart is deceitful above all things."* (Jeremiah 17:9) Or is it?

I pose this question not to refute the word of God, but rather to bring this Scripture into some "context" with this new and better covenant of our redemption. First we must grasp and understand that when the Bible uses the word heart in such circumstances outside of the literal use, it is referring to the mind of a man. The will, thoughts, desires; the core of a man. The soul. Jeremiah said that this was deceitful because everything about it was wicked, and swayed by the Deceiver. As I said, we were purely natural and naturally motivated, carnally speaking. But the Scriptures declared a new thing, or better said, a "renewed" thing happened with our baptism in Christ. We received the mind of Christ himself.

Remember, the spirit-man died as soon as he touched this physical realm. Everything about him died. The spirit, itself, was essentially nonexistent leaving only the soul of the man, ruled by wickedness, and the flesh, which consisted basically of spectacularly organized dirt. The *huge* problem is, nothing was left in the dirt to keep it unsusceptible to death, and everything correlated with that. Flesh was rectified, even physically, as briefly stated previously, but that is completely irrelevant if the soul of a man is not changed. Christ made it clear that even the thought-life of a man constitutes as a sinful action. (This actually makes perfect sense considering we were made likened unto the image of God, and the Bible declares His very thoughts come to pass.) So death would once more inhabit our very being, nullifying our spirit, and corrupting our flesh. But Christ exchanged our old mind for the very mind of God Almighty, resulting in the very nature of God ever present before us and in us. (Philippians 2:5, 1 Corin. 2:16) As John said,

> *Beloved, I wish above all things that thou mayest prosper and be in health, **even as thy soul prospereth.** 3 John 1:2 (KJV)*

So I think we've covered all the problems that were responsible, or at least considered responsible, for our habits of sin. Satan, the Deceiver, has been defeated, and stripped of all authority and power, rendering him impotent, not to mention, his competition (us) has the Life and power of God flowing through them. Remember Christ said, *"all authority in heaven and in earth is given unto me."*

Flesh, anyway you cut it, has been rectified, and sin/sinful nature has been done away with in us as sure as Satan's power has been eradicated from him.

His (Christ') very mind and subsequent nature rules in us. So my question now is, what could possibly cause you, the redeemed of the LORD, to sin?

> *Aw @#$%! This fool dun went too far now. Predestination is one thing. But you tryin'a tell me... You sayin' that we ain't supposed to sin... That you don't sin... Ever?*

> *You know what? I was gonna call you crazy, but*

here you go. Here's an actual Scripture for you. 1ˢᵗ John 1:8, and I quote, "If we say that we have no sin, we deceive ourselves, and the truth is not in us." See that, man. You ain't only lyin' to us, you lyin' to ya self. I'm done. This fool is a liar!

(This *would* normally be one of those points when Christians get ignorant)

First thing I would say to that is, "N*gga, who you talkin to?!" I'm playing. Just a little humor. Sorry if I offended some of the "holy" folk out there. That is <u>not</u> a word I use.

Seriously though, the first thing I would say to that, is read the first verse of Chapter 2. *"These things I write you that you sin not...?"* Secondly I'm glad you're already in that book because we were actually headed to Chapter 3.

I spoke to you of faith in the previous chapter and tried to make it plain as to how faith is "gathered." Well these Scriptures have been Life-giving to me, as I believe it will be to you.

1ˢᵗ John 3:4-10

⁴Whosoever committeth sin transgresseth also the law, for sin is transgression of the law. ⁵And ye know that he (Christ) was manifested to take away our sins; and in him is no sin. ⁶Whosoever abitheth in him (Christ) sinneth not: whosoever sinneth hath not seen him, neither known him. ⁷Little children, let no man deceive you: he that doeth righteousness is righteous, even as he (Christ) is righteous. ⁸He that committeth sin is of the devil; for the

> *devil sinneth from the beginning. For this purpose the Son of God was manifested, that he might destroy the works of the devil. ⁹Whosoever is born of God doth not commit sin; for his (God) seed remaineth in him; and he cannot sin, because he is born of God. ¹⁰In this the children of God are manifest, and the children of the devil; whosoever doeth not righteousness is not of God, neither he that loveth not his bother.*

> **You can't take that "literally," or at least, it can't completely apply to us because... like it said, "he who abides in Christ sins not," and we don't always abide in Christ. No one's perfect.**

Actually, Christ was [and is] perfect and that's the whole point. Romans 8:29 states:

> *For whom he did foreknow, he also did predestinate to be conformed to the image of his Son, that he (Christ) might be the firstborn among many brethren.*

God foreordained that we who believed would be conformed to look just like Christ (inwardly obviously) through rebirth, as Christ leading the way as the firstborn from death amongst many born of the same womb. Or should I say "tomb"... (too corny...) Hence God requires perfection from us just as He has from His only begotten Son.

> *Be ye therefore perfect, <u>even</u> as your Father which is in heaven is perfect.* Matthew 5:48 (KJV)

As well, that statement about abiding in Christ that we may not sin, and us not always abiding, is quite a self-destructing one. The notion that we don't always abide in him, or that we stray sometimes, don't walk the "straight and narrow," etc., implicates sin, obviously. The only problem with that is, once you abide in him, how do you sin, seeing that *"whosoever abideth in him (Christ) sinneth not?"*

Well, I believe that's more the practice of sinning, or habitual sin, if you would. He does not sin consistently.

I see. So the fact that you just read that whoever is born of God does not commit sin, and **cannot** sin, because the seed of God, which is Christ, remains in him and in Christ <u>is no sin</u>, and he that commits sin <u>is of the devil</u>, and... Should I keep going? Ok, we'll assume that he <u>did not</u> mean what he said. Here's a question.

How much sin makes you a habitual sinner? Or how much do you have to commit sin daily before it's considered practicing? How many times acceptably fits into "not sinning" within a week's span? How about we go as far as once a year? It's funny... New Year's, Christmas, Valentine's Day? I'm fairly certain that these events happen consistently.

No, see God, as I said before, is very particular about His words, and doesn't need revisions and interpretations from our finite minds.

> *Well I've yet to see a sinless person. As a matter of fact, what's the point of asking for forgiveness as the Bible tells us to do if we "can't sin." John even says, 'If we confess our sins, he is faithful and just to forgive us our sins and to cleanse us from all unrighteous.'* **(1 John 1:9)** *So tell me, where are these sinless believers at, while the rest us, who <u>apparently</u> aren't sinless, and can't seem to accomplish this feat, are told to confess our sins that "don't exist?"*

Well, you may have got me there. (Obviously not, because what idiot would kill his own points in his own book.) Let's go back to the 1ˢᵗ John 1:8 verse you brought up previously, because they are connecting and therefore correlating verses, and I haven't really addressed that directly.

"If we say that we have no sin, we deceive ourselves, and the truth is not in us." One hundred percent correct. Consider a point we all will agree on (as believers at least), we all have sinned in this life, especially considering, if we've done nothing more than been born, we came to this world in it (sin). *("... shapen in iniquity"* Psalm 51:5).

Which leads to the next verse, but we'll have to look at the end of it, intently. *"If we confess our sins, he is faithful and just to forgive..,"* implying we first recognize our sin, the One we've sinned against, and the same One who can and will forgive it. Sounds to me like our "profession of faith." But, look at the "finally". *"He is faithful and just to forgive us our sins and to cleanse us from <u>all</u> unrighteousness."* I don't know your definition of "all," but last time I checked, the word "all" was all-encompassing. Past, present, and potential future. So if He's cleansed it, wiped it clean, all of it, what is this sin you are asking forgiveness for after the first time you asked?

I started to consider this, after I began to study 1st John 3, looking for some biblical assertion to confirm this concept of continually asking forgiveness for sin through this life in which sin has been eradicated the first time you repented of such ways.

I say unto you, that likewise joy shall be in heaven over one sinner that repenteth, more than over ninety and nine just persons, ***which need no repentance****.* Luke 15:7 (KJV)

And please don't try to say I've taken this out of context, because the statement is declaratory. It can stand by itself. You'd have no problem quoting the verse by itself to someone coming to Christ. (Not that I would either) If a man, moving by the Spirit of God, cannot go without sin, then obviously it is not possible for an individual to not need repentance.

*Therefore let us go on and get past the elementary stage in the teachings and doctrine of Christ (the Messiah), advancing steadily toward the completeness and perfection that belong to spiritual maturity. Let us **not** again be laying the foundation of repentance and abandonment of dead works (dead formalism) and of the faith [by which you turned] to God* (Heb. 6:1) AMP

As to your ability to achieve perfection… let me tell you, or propose to you a scenario. (Long chapter, huh?)

You have an extremely wealthy uncle who died. Though you don't know him, in his will he left you a sum of $100,000. Only problem is you are not aware of this uncle, let alone his will.

…Is the money still yours?

I'll answer it for you, though I'm relatively certain you know the answer. This is not a deep philosophical question. The answer is most certainly, yes. You have legal right to ownership of the full sum (minus taxes, etc.). However, there still remains an issue, and a big one at that. You cannot operate with something you are not aware you have. So it is with the Testimony and word of God.

> *^{23}For if any be a hearer of the word, and not a doer, he is like unto a man beholding his natural face in a glass (mirror): ^{24}For he beholdeth himself, and goeth his way, and straightway forgetteth what manner of man he was.* James 1:23-24 (KJV)

This Scripture is a testimony to the location of these sinless people and this "feat" that seems unattainable. This is why faith is so crucial and the only thing that can satisfy the requirement of God. There are two key points to this verse; *"any [man],"* and what this man is likened to. "Any [man]." Not Christian or believers, or the righteous, or any other term the Bible uses to distinguish us from them. (That being the redeemed as opposed to the unsaved.) Well get back to this point shortly.

What is he likened to? It *doesn't* say if this man hears the Word, the Truth, etc. and doesn't do it, he's a sinner, a heathen, wretched. It says this man saw himself reflected and actually forgot what he looked like. What manner of man he is. His image; his likeness; his character. The word of God, the Bible is actually a mirror, informing us what we already look like. Not some image we are to achieve or 'strive' for, but what we already are.

So where does "any man" come into play?

> *Therefore as by the offence of one judgment came upon all men to condemnation; even so by the righteousness of one the free gift came upon all men unto justification of life.* Romans 5:18 (KJV)

So what is this saying? One (Adam) committed an offence which brought judgment and condemnation upon all men. In this same manner of acting "one for all," Christ's righteous act has brought the free gift of justification to all men. Do you understand, because this is not as obvious as it may seem? If it is as obvious as it should be, you have to start considering some things. Adam sinned, subsequently we all inherited sin and death. It wasn't a choice of ours; we were born into it. This verse is saying in this same way, by Christ's righteous act (crucifixion and resurrection), justification and life was inherited by all men. Which implies that, all men are saved. (Keep reading)

Buddy! What are you smokin'?! Even if that were true, you're contradicting yourself with the whole predestination bit. But go on. I gotta hear you get out of this one, or "explain" this one.

I appreciate your conviction, though it's another thing you're blowing off with no explanation other than, "You're wrong" despite the Scripture right in your face. But... the conclusion that all men are saved and redeemed would be 100 percent <u>INCORRECT</u>. So good for you. However we still have an issue, because, once again, the Scripture clearly says what it says. This is where "any man" comes into play. Faith, the perceived and believed revelation knowledge of the Truth. You cannot operate in justification of life, unless first you perceive this justification and believe you've received it. The Scripture puts it this way:

> *How then shall they call on him in whom they have not believed? and how shall they believe in him of whom they have not heard?* Romans 10:14 (KJV)

All men have been justified. All sin, up to and including those of them that are presently just and unjust, and those to come, was taken on Christ upon the cross. The problem is though men have been given legal right to righteousness, so many don't know and or have seemingly forgotten what God has created them to be. This is why it say "*any* [man]." And this is why the Bible say, *"without faith it is impossible to please him (God)."* Therefore, the just don't live trying to be godly, or building up their holiness. They live by faith. That which is invisible and that which can only be accomplished by God. This is where all these sinless people dwell. They live in Christ through faith. "We walk not by sight (what we are 'seeing') but by faith." (2 Corin. 5:7) Just as we were called to. This is the power of faith.

I am crucified with Christ: nevertheless I live; **yet not I, but Christ liveth in me**: *and the life which I now live in the flesh I* *live by the **faith** in the Son of God, who loved me, and gave himself for me.* Galatians 2:20 (KJV)

Yet not I... *Yet not I*, but CHRIST. And this life being lived constitutes by belief in something that I don't have to see first. And the powerful thing is that faith eventually has to manifests outwardly for it to ever have been real faith. It must come to pass. In this case not as an event in the future but "the life I now live." The life I'm presently living.

Every where I look in the Word, all godliness, and all righteous exploits are done "through Christ." Through Christ, through Christ... It's everywhere I look. God's very blessing and favor towards us is always "through Christ," "in Christ." Like the only way He can reach us even now, even in the redeemed state, is through His Son. And we act like Christ is some door we go through or a bridge we cross to get to the Father rather than understanding he's much more comparable to the room, or the world we step into. Let me show you something.

³For you died, and your life is now hidden with Christ in God. ⁴When Christ, who is your life, appears, then you also will appear with him in glory. Colossians 3:3-4 (NIV)

Paul said, "You may not be aware, but let me clarify some things for you. You died. This already happened. I know you've been fighting with some things, but it was really a lie. That's what you've been fighting with. You are actually, presently, hidden away in Christ."

This gives some silly perspective and clarity to *"I'm seated with Christ in heavenly places."* (Ephesians 2:6) "Me-time" or "My life," all that stuff, it's done, and praise God! Fret no more. The next time 'you' have to make a 'personal appearance' is when Christ reveals himself in glory.

Well I don't get it? Who's living in me? Who am I? Who is this that I see every day?

The same person you claim is living in you every time you tell someone about Him. It is His very Spirit. You didn't know it was actually quite literal every time you heard someone say "your life for His." But the Scriptures tell us, that's what He had in mind. "The seed has to die to produce a harvest after its kind. So if I die, they'll die too. If they die, obviously in entirety; if they die the same way I have, that will free them from any claim (demand or ownership) the kingdom of darkness has over them and I will "translate" (reproduce a specific entity into a different form while retaining the original meaning or function) into my kingdom of light. The same way they used to be 'slaves to sin' they will be "slaves to righteousness." (Romans 6:18) They won't be able to stop themselves. As sin lived in and through them, so will I now. And there will be Me's everywhere." This is why he says, *"(You) be of good cheer, for I have overcome the world."* (John 16:33) I've already done it. Now the world is subject to me. *"All authority in heaven and in earth..."* Even as I live through you. The only thing that is required for this whole thing to work is the very faith you use when you knowingly or unknowingly made this oath with God. The power lies in the faith. So faith must increase for Him to increase in you. But God said I got that too. He is *"the author (creator) and finisher (completer) of our faith."* (Hebrews 12:2)

So Paul goes on to say in his letter:

[5]Put to death, therefore, whatever belongs to your earthly nature: sexual immorality, impurity, lust, evil desires and greed, which is idolatry. [6]Because of these, the wrath of God is coming. [7]You used to walk in these ways, in the life you once lived. [8]But now you must rid yourselves of all such things as these: anger, rage, malice, slander, and filthy language from your lips. [9]Do not lie to each other, since you have taken off your old self with its practices [10]and have put on the new self, which is being renewed

in knowledge in the image of its Creator. Colossians 3:5-10 (NIV)

Paul said, "Put this stuff to death. Rid yourself of these things." But notice what He said in the middle of it. "You used to walk in this, **but since** you have taken off your old self... I know what I'm 'seeing' you do, but the **REALITY** is that by faith... (*faith comes by hearing, and hearing by the Word of God*) Now that you know, put it away. That was the old man. The new you is remade moment by moment by learning about the likeness and character of the Creator who has chosen you as His vessel, His temple.

Therefore let us go on and get past the elementary stage in the teachings and doctrine of Christ (the Messiah), advancing steadily toward the completeness and perfection that belong to spiritual maturity. Let us not again be laying the foundation of repentance and abandonment of dead works (dead formalism) and of the faith [by which you turned] to God Hebrews 6:1 (Amp)

The Pissed off Writings of a Prophet

Chapter 6:
The Fivefold Ministry:
Everyone's a Pastor

This topic has been, kind of, "irking" me for a while. Maybe because no one seems to notice, nobody cares to notices, no one even knows…? Whatever it may be, for whatever reason, it seems anyone [generally speaking] involved in ministry that is not primarily in missions work is a pastor, or operates under the same paradigm as your "prototypical" pastor. Only problem is that according to the Word, Christ has set forth five specific ministry giftings, which we have aptly called the fivefold ministry gifting, offices, etc.

Well, if the gospel be preached, is it really that big a deal?

- The first obvious answer is that God thinks it's important enough to inform us of this and set it into place, so yes, it must have great significance to it.
- The Scriptures that I believe we gain the most insight to this "enterprise" (for a lack of a better word) speaks quite directly to the function and purpose of the offices:

> ^{11}*And he gave some, apostles; and some, prophets; and some, evangelists; and some, pastors and teachers;* ^{12}*For the perfecting of the saints, for the work of the ministry, for the edifying of the body of Christ:* ^{13}*Till we all come in the unity of the faith, and of the knowledge of the Son of God, unto a perfect man, unto the measure of the stature of the fulness of Christ:* Eph. 4:11-13

The whole point of these giftings and anointing, is that the whole body of Christ maybe brought into perfection individually, as well as a unit in the faith in Christ (kills the denomination concept), and as it apply to his body operating in its complete fullness.

I must also bring attention to another ordinance because as a leader goes, so does his following, and there is disorder and subsequent chaos in many aspect of the Church today that has not been before. 1 Corin. 12:28 states:

> *And God has appointed in the church first apostles, second prophets, third teachers, then miracles, then gifts of healing, helping, administrating, and various kinds of tongues.* (KJV)

So this is what's bothering me. Why is that everywhere I go, I see two pastors to a block, some with special titles, such as apostle or prophet, but essentially "shepherds" of a flock, that do nothing more that deliver a sermon every Sunday, and the couple randomly designated days during the week. Where are the apostles and prophets, the critical gifts God has placed in these individual, to build up His body?

Rest assured, this is not a crack against all pastors, or the ministry of a pastor. Truthfully, I wonder how many "pastors" that have been called to the ministry, have not stepped into the fullness of their gifting, due to the fact that all we know today is how to be a pastor of a church. So, if we may, let's dissect these ministries and at least get some basic truth, not assumptions and "tradition," on these matters.

Apostles:

Apostolos (Greek) -

A *delegate*; specifically an *ambassador* of the Gospel; officially a *commissioner* of Christ ("apostle"), (with miraculous powers): - apostle, messenger, he that is sent. (Also from the Greek word which means "to be set apart.")

Now, I don't know everything, but there's the assumption, that because there are accounts of apostles seen in the New Testament starting churches, this is the telling sign and function of what apostles are supposed to do. (Wow... I wonder how stupid we can get as human beings before our bodies stop working and we die? That's like saying, since I saw an employee at work washing his hands on a few occasions, to be a legitimate employee in any work environment, you **have** to occasionally wash your hands.)

There is also the much scarier claim that one can only be an apostle if you've seen Christ personally; therefore, the last apostle to walk this Earth was Paul. However, a glaring issue with that claim (based off the Scriptures from Ephesians previously stated) is the fact that I along with so many others disagree with that. That alone is a pretty obvious contradiction in "unity of the faith." No unity in faith, by all of Christ's body, constitutes that the ministry of an apostle must continue.

So what is the ministry of an apostle? I'm going to do something that so many pastors don't. I'm going to tell you that from my wisdom, there's *only* so much I know, and I am not going to try extend myself further than what I know solely for the sake of looking like I know what I'm talking about. But there are a few things I do.

One, the apostles ministry is by authority and gifting the greatest and the highest of callings concerning the fivefold. Of the different ministries, everyone seems to have some basic clarity in function and gifting, but the apostle's gifting, his anointing, seems to be in the actual fact that is he chosen and sent as an ambassador of God. So what is the significance of that?

An ambassador is one who is essentially an extension of the one who sent him, and is thus received as the one who sent him would be. The ambassador holds only the thoughts and opinion of the sender; he is not permitted to convey any of his own. So essentially this would apply to all Christians, and that is my point. The definition conveys that an apostle is anointed above all others to represent the King here on earth. Not that a man should be glorified as God, but he is gifted to act accordingly as God's delegate, and is chosen to be received accordingly, as such.

Side note: Women are fully capable and within divine right to be gifted in the ministry of an apostle or any other, permitted she is called, just as a male would be. (Read your Bible.)

Prophet:

Prophētēs (Greek) -

A foreteller

From *pro* - fore, prior to, in front of, above, ever;

And *phemi* - to show or make known one's thoughts

This ministry is very close to me, more so than I can convey with words, because it is the gifting God has given me, and due to the gift, it has shaped me spiritually in a way, I believe only another prophet could fully understand. (That could quite possibly be same for all God's ministry gifting.)

Many believe that it is the duty of a prophet to make known future events, but that is in actuality, only a "by-product," if you will, of the gifting.

[If I can speak as a representative of the prophetic ministry...] While the other ministries seem to have the focus of God concerning directly the service to the people, a prophet's *focus* is not so much concerned with people as it is with God Himself. The prophet is continually trying to "pick" the mind of God, continually searching God out to understand what He wants and why He would want it this way, and how He would do it, and what He wouldn't do, and what He's done before, and when He's going to do again, if He's going to do it again, and the list goes on.

It is not a matter so much of "Father, show me what to do with Your people," as it is "Father, show me You." This is why when you read biblical accounts of the prophets, they seem so often to be by themselves or amongst each other. They kind of appear at the appointed time and just as soon "vanish."

Please don't get it twisted. As though I were saying that the prophet does not concern himself with the affairs of men, because if you are truly seeking God, you find out, that's what is on His mind. His love and care for men is so often overwhelming. (Jeremiah, the great Old Testament prophet, has been known by many as the "weeping prophet.") My point is, instead of having the "burden" to concern ourselves with the _"fill in the blank"_ of the people God would charge to us (our care), our energies are devoted to the task of ministering to God.

The best way I can describe this is like a point Paul makes about marriages.

> *33But the married man is anxious about worldly things, how to please his wife, 34and his interests are divided. And the unmarried or betrothed woman is anxious about the things of the Lord, how to be holy in body and spirit. But the married woman is anxious about worldly things, how to please her husband.* 1 Cor. 7:33-34 (ESV)

So the prophet's ministry to the body becomes the task of making known or showing forth what's on God's mind. God says He makes known the end from the beginning (Isaiah 46:10), and He never does anything without first revealing it (Amos 3:7), so subsequently the prophet often speaks of things to come. This is where the understanding that a prophet sees and speaks the future comes from. And this is why I said before, that specific part of the gifting is essentially a by-product, and not a primary function.

Evangelist:

Euaggelistēs (Greek) -

A preacher of the gospel

From *eu* - good

And *aggelos* - messenger, bringer of tidings

I can definitely say that this is much easier for me to define than the previous two. Simply, the evangelist is anointed to carry the good news of Jesus Christ as a messenger, which is similar in obvious ways to the ministry of an apostle. One main focus of this ministry, that I believe the Church has done right by, is the fact the one does not come to a messenger but a messenger goes where he must and delivers the message. So is the function of an evangelist.

Pastor:

Poimēn (Greek)-

A shepherd

Pastor (English)-

O great one! (Joking)

I will be careful as to not get extreme and become disrespectful of this truly wonderful ministry. If not for pastors, quite seriously, where would we be? Pastors have been charged with the task of overseeing their flock, and so many times, that means fighting off the wolves, and/or leaving the rest of the flock just to save one stray that has went off on their own accord.

One does not get to take breaks from shepherding, lest a sheep be destroyed. And given the fact that God's shepherds are merely stewards of the Master's flocks, if a sheep be lost, reasonably the steward will have to answer for it.

Though the shepherd and his sheep may move and circle around regionally for "green pasture," the pastor remains a local governing entity and authority with those sheep that have been place in his charge.

Teacher:

Didaskalos (Greek)

Instructor; doctor, master, teacher

I don't think this one can get simpler. One who is anointed to instruct, and instruct as one who has mastered or doctored their respective "discipline(s)." Obviously all being for the Kingdom.

I mentioned earlier that I will not disrespect the ministry of a pastor, and I will not, but I must issue this warning, to our pastors as well as the rest of the body, because an arrogance has crept into this ministry, not specifically concerning the individuals but the position as an institution.

Pastors are not the head, or epitome of the ministry as a whole, nor are they the cornerstone. And I am not referring to Christ himself being our head; or the pope, bishop, cardinal, deacon status thing going on denominationally. (I'm not saying that stuff is necessarily bad either). Whether it has been the patrons or the pastors themselves that have exalted this office so high, I don't know, but the pastor has become "judge, jury, and executioner" so to speak. If the pastor says it, "he's the pastor and the highest authority of men." Pastors themselves are starting to believe if you don't have a title and a church, "then I must be greater than you." But remember, He has appointed **first** apostles, then prophets, *then* teachers and such. So be carefully, man of God, what you say and who you are saying it to, because that someone you are talking to *may be* an apostle or prophet, or maybe just the next one God has set apart and chosen to carry His word and anointing in a greater measure. You are not the final or ultimate authority among men. He has given giftings and grace to men in measures, not to make one better than the other, but to establish order and hierarchy in *His* Kingdom.

I recall, not so long ago, a man I esteem highly in the faith (a pastor), declared to his congregation that God does not call novices to the ministry of a prophet, as though there is some graduation process to reach the level of prophet, or any other ministry office. Concerning many of those mentioned in the Bible as prophets, from Moses to Isaiah to Jeremiah, such have expressed inadequacy when first called to their ministries. God Himself says to Jeremiah, *"before I formed you in the womb, I ordained you a prophet to the nations."* Ministry gifts/offices are not earned and merited by men from men, but are preordained and chosen by the Most High. Just as a child-king doesn't chose or conqueror his kingdom into submission, he is made king by his birth right and is respected and honored as king by all regardless of "merit."

I must reiterate that I am not here to attack pastors; they get attacked enough, which will happen anytime you stand up for God and godliness. But I see that we as Christians are trying to figure out why we see these powerful individuals here and there but as a whole, we are seemingly quite sketchy. Many people use the term "churchianity." I won't, basically because I don't know what that term means to each individually.

We have a paradigm, a template in "Today's Christianity" that says to be a good Christian no matter who or what you are, you have to find a "pastor" and church [building] and go to that church at least every Sunday. **PLEASE LISTEN TO ME CAREFULLY.** I am not saying that this in and of itself is a bad thing at all. I have a church (which I work in) and a wonderful pastor. To say she is wonderful is quite the understatement ['cause she's a **MONSTER**- in a very good way], but we'll get to all that later. My issue is that we act like this is *THE* God-prescribed, God-ordained template, and that any form of Christian living that is more than a slight variance of this is "not in order."

Get me straight please. There are definitely a lot of godless happenings and organization, groups, etc. claiming that they are doing God work in the name of Christ. I am not advocating anarchy in the Kingdom or some "I don't need any man whatsoever to *ever* lead me cause I got Jesus" type of thing. Maybe if I propose some questions it'll help paint a picture.

Who was Peter's 'pastor'? Who was Paul's 'pastor'? What 'church' did John 'pastor'? Where was Matthew's 'church' located? Who 'preached' when all the apostles came together? What day did they schedule 'service'? What time was it at? Did Barnabas 'preach' during 'Bible study'? How many 'church members' did Timothy have at his 'church'? What was the name of the 'church' in Corinth? Was there one or more? Who were the 'pastors' there?

Where did we get this idea that I have to find my 'pastor' and we'll meet every Sunday at the designated 'church' where nobody amongst these group of believers but 'pastor' truly knows what God has in mind? Every Sunday you'd better be at the designated 'church' and listen to the only one in this group of believers that truly knows what God is saying. And this is Christian living.

You want to do something for God? *Did 'Pastor' sign off? Did you do it the way 'Pastor' does it?*

Did God tell you to do something? *Oh no, He didn't. 'Pastor' said we got Bible study tonight...* and everything he thinks super cedes anything God can personally say to you. You ain't figured it out yet? Your Christian life is dictated solely by a singular man's grasp of what God is saying.

Seek God for yourself? *Why? 'Pastor' was already told what everybody's supposed to be doing.*

There is a Scripture that most know but have not considered any kind understanding of it other than the same partial explanation given across churches today.

Not forsaking the assembling of ourselves together, as the manner of some is; but exhorting one another: and so much the more, as ye see the day approaching. Hebrews 10:25 (KJV)

Under what stretch of the imagination does that interpret: Go to church on every Sunday so Pastor can preach to you?

Exhorting one another…?

Exhort- to urge, advise, or caution earnestly; admonish urgently.

Hopefully the pastor of the church is exhorting, and praise God for that, truly. What are the rest of us doing? Exhorting Pastor by saying "Amen"? ***Amen, Pastor! Amen!*** That's our exhortation?

The Bible says we overcome by His blood, and the word of **our** testimony. (Rev. 12:11)

How can the Body be empowered, how can It overcome, if the only ones 'entitled' to testify are 'pastors'. If someone else wants to "exhort" they better first get in 'pastors' good graces, and don't let them 'exhort' more than 3 minutes twice a year 'cause if pastor don't get them, everybody else's looks will make sure they know they're "out of order."

Try taking the gospel outside of the church? *Did Pastor ok it? Who ordained you? AAAANNNT! Nope! Out of order!*

Also, who decides how often assembling is constituted as assembling. Who told us we have to meet every Sunday. Who picked Sunday? The seventh day, the Sabbath is Saturday. Who told us Sunday was *enough*?

That's why we have 'Testimony Tuesday' Bible Studies and 'Fill Us Up Friday' Service. Who told us *that* was enough? To keep it real the Bible says that they assembled **daily**. *Well we can't do that anymore. Times have changed.*

Maybe that's true, but who decided that? God or 'pastor'? Or even the congregation?

I've said all this and I'm sure that at this point, it seem like I'm opposed to church and I tell you the truth ("Verily, verily, I say unto you) I am not. I am opposed to going to church for church-sake, like we're obligated to the building. I am opposed to holding firmly to a very specific concept having no Biblical representation and never actually having sought out God to see if He wanted something more. The same thing all the time, empowering nothing but feelings, emotionalism, and a man's reputation, and doing it for no other reason than that's what we've always done. The problem is, it hasn't always been this way. We know this because we have no biblical reference. For something so structured and rigid, how it is that we can't find anything like it mentioned? Wherever it came from, I do believe it originated out of goodness and wisdom, and I am not saying that I believe it is obsolete. I believe by failing to seek God in all things, even individually, and being united corporately by *His* one Spirit, we have made His ability to move in His fullness null and void by vain tradition. (Mark 7:13)

I, myself, do have an amazing pastor that I have submitted myself to. Not because of her handle, the fact that she has a church building, not because she went to school, not because she has godly people 'vouching' for her. Twenty-Ten was easily the most difficult, trying time of my life, and I can said in truth, that if it were not for the Christ in HER continually feeding and admonishing, I *could not* see myself having made it though. I do not believe I would have. But I have not submitted myself to her and her ministry even because of that. I submit myself to her simply because He has established her with His anointing and *commanded* me, that as long as He sees fit, I will serve with her in whatever fashion He deems beneficial to the Kingdom.

To all those in the "ministry," to all those called and anointed in the gifting of these "offices.":

The Kingdom we belong to and the manner in which it runs is completely contrary to the world system we came from. Those in authority are not called to "rule" but to serve. (Mark 10:42-45) The higher the calling the lower the stature. And just incase you doubt that.

> [9]*For I think that God has exhibited us apostles as last of all, like men sentenced to death, because we have become a spectacle to the world, to angels, and to men.* [10]*We are fools for Christ's sake, but you are wise in*

Christ. We are weak, but you are strong. You are held in honor, but we in disrepute. ^{11}To the present hour we hunger and thirst, we are poorly dressed and buffeted and homeless, ^{12}and we labor, working with our own hands. When reviled, we bless; when persecuted, we endure; ^{13}when slandered, we entreat. We have become, and are still, like the scum of the world, the refuse of all things. ^{14}I do not write these things to make you ashamed, but to admonish you as my beloved children. 1 Corin. 4:9-14 (KJV)

The Bible says as believers we are to consider others to be better than ourselves. (Philippians 2:3) What does that say for those of us called to lead? The least among us shall be great, and the greatest the least. (Luke 9:48)

We're actually getting worst than the world. *The world doesn't respect us and that's fine. They laugh at us at best most of the time. But in the "church," they **will** respect me there.* The problem is we don't really want respect. We want fear, *'cause fear will keep them in line. In their place of order.* The problem is no one is supposed to fear you or any other man. They are called to fear God. Your ministry is not your own. It is God's. If they don't respect you and honor you; if no one respects and honor you, that's fine. The only honor you are worthy of in the first place is the honoring of **Christ** in you. It is not your responsibility to gather honor from men. The honor of men is due to God. The Bible says in due time **God** will exalt you. (1 Peter 5:6) Even if He would use men to do His bidding, it is still in Him and through Him that honor comes.

This is why we are crazy about handles. *I need to have my proper respect and my handle designates me from everyone else, it separates me, it sets me above.* Tell me, when do you ever see a handle attached to anyone's name in the Bible..? Ever..? Maybe I have to look again, but I do not recall it. The Bible definitely lists gifts and callings of the individuals but no one ever calls to another under this type of protocol. "Apostle *This,*" "Prophet *That,*" "Evangelist *XYZ.*" This stuff wouldn't be bad if it didn't come from a place of arrogance. Why do I *have* to call you that? Why are you offended if I don't? Was this anointing accomplished by means of your own or was it solely by His grace? I'm not saying that the people with these handles are genuinely arrogant. Most I know aren't. But it is a whole means of exalting oneself amongst men. God knows what you are. He gave you the gift. So who are you running around, broadcasting, name-dropping for? I'm not even saying you have to hide it. But Peter and Paul were "Peter" and "Paul." Why do you have to be called Pastor? Heck, they would even call Peter, "Cephas," like a nickname. And before you go into "Cephas means rocks in Aramaic" informing me of what I already know and proving my point for me, consider a nickname is normally just a variance of the initial name.

We must understand that it's not "ministry workers" and laymen —AKA everyone else that doesn't matter. Service to God is service to God regardless of who's doing it. Don't think, because you get to stand up in front of a crowd, and people listen to you merely *relay* a message *that's not even yours,* these people who are called to relay this very same Word you spoke to them, to others who don't know, somehow you are now more than them. Somehow *you* are supposed to be exalted above another in **God's** Kingdom because **God** gifted you to manifest **Him** to others that need to know **Him**. Tell me, who else in His Kingdom does that *not* describe? But this is "church-culture." Everyone knows how to behave in "church" but wonders why we can't find no "Kingdom." (Excuse the double-negative) No power or authority over anything but each other.

I was recently listening to a man of God preach, a prophet, and this man was the real deal, truly. The man knew your name, birthday, address, social security number, bank account number, etc. It seemed pretty evident that this man walked in humility. He did not flaunt the gift. And those of us who are mature in Christ know that men do not simply operate with this kind of sensitivity to the Spirit… Put it this way, regardless of what we may think of men, the Holy Spirit does not move any old kind of way in those whose lifestyle does not reflect godly virtues. I'm simply stating that I do not believe at all this man to be an arrogant man. But he was recounting a story of when he went to minister at a particular church. The church sent someone, probably a deacon, to pick him up from the airport I believe. When the man arrived to pick him up, he stepped out of the car and went to greet the prophet with a "high-five, shake-up hug, 'what's up, man?" type of deal. The man of God basically responded with a kind of "no buddy, you got the wrong one" type of deal. I don't believe at all that he was trying to be rude, and initially I was thinking to myself, along with basically everyone else present, "Yeah, that fool was crazy. You don't do that. That ain't really any type of proper etiquette." But it sat with me for a while until I considered, if that was Jesus, how would he have received the man? Would he have responded, "Negro, don't you know I'm the King of kings." Or maybe it would have been closer to, "Greetings my brother, beloved of my Father," as he hugged his brother.

The problem was that man of God has been conditioned in a "church-culture" and consequently his conviction tells him that this manner of reception wasn't "right," that it's "out of order." But if Christ would not receive a man that way, **WHAT IN THE**

HELL MAKE YOU THINK *YOU* CAN? And I truly mean to use the word "hell" because that thought process ain't coming from God's side. (I am not as angry as that statement may seem) I've heard over and over from pastors "I'm not your friend, I'm Pastor." My response is, and I say this in love (that's what we say when we're about to criticize, but do not want to offend), how completely silly is that? Jesus said *"Greater love has no man than this, that a man lay down his life for his friend."* (John 15:13) If Christ considers that his greatest love has been shown to those he calls his "friend" by actually giving up his life for me, how can you possibly think you are moving in the love of Christ toward your brother, and I am somehow *not* your friend? Is that a joke? Normally, I hear them say, "You don't want me to be your friend because friends won't tell you when you are wrong." Yeah, if you're in the world. Cowards won't tell you when you're wrong. Somehow though, God has *mysteriously* managed to accomplish this "impossible" task throughout the entire history of mankind.

The point of this chapter is that we have to get out of this solitary way of doing things because it's the only way we know, and step into [Holy] Spirit-driven lives in [Holy] Spirit-guided order, loosing His Spirit to move in every facet He is capable of [which is limitless].

Chapter 7
Hell: A Two Part Saga

P<u>art I</u>:
I had a conversation, a few years ago, with a friend of mine (who is a passionate believer) about the Mel Gibson film, The Passion of the Christ. (Don't know of a more impactful movie <u>ever</u> released.) The movie had just been released in theaters; he had seen it already, and I had plans very soon to view it myself. I asked him what he thought about it, because as many of you know, there were huge talks, and even advertisements, about the high graphic nature of this depiction of Christ's crucifixion. Obviously, I was very excited to see the movie in general. But he kind of surprised me with his response to my question. He said he didn't really know what to think about it, because obviously he enjoyed the message, but he thought the amount of graphic violence was a bit overdone (fictional), and somewhat ridiculous. Basically, no man, that is to say no human, could have survived, let alone, continued on under such torture. He simply would have died along the way. I tell you what. He was right on one point.

I think about that conversation all the time for many different reasons, but it occurs to me, more and more, that not many people really know the literal "hell" Christ went through, from his arrest to his death. I'm not claiming to know every single detail that happened during that time span, but I do know things many people are shocked to hear, and one thing in particular that most people don't stop to consider too often, if at all. My purpose of giving the following biblical/historical account is that, maybe, someone will begin to consider these things themselves, and if for no other reasons concerning the marvelous things God has done for you, *this* could be enough to fully yield your life to him, as he did for you.

The story begins at night in a garden where Jesus went to pray. Jesus was not alone though. His wonderful friends [and disciples] where there too, but they might as well *not* have been. They had a long day and were a bit too tired to stay awake and pray with him. And this time of prayer was no ordinary time. He had never gone to the Father like this before. He was so stressed over what was to come, that he actually implored the Father, if there was some way out, some alternative way, **something** other than what he had to do. Something he's known he would have to do before the worlds were even made. Something he continually stated publically as his very purpose for coming to us. Well, his sorrow was so overwhelming; he was in such agony, that the capillaries surrounding his sweat glands burst causing "great drops" of blood to seep through his pores. (Very rare condition by the way.) Yet he continued on.

Then comes his arrest and betrayal. These soldiers are so deranged by spirits, that they actually seized him, despite the fact that they would witness first hand a terrifying phenomenon, just moments before. See when they came looking for him, his voice carried so much power in proclamation, "I Am [the One you seek]," it knocked them all to the ground.

The men he had shared his life with for the last 3 years, continually reaffirming to them that he was the Son of God, continually building their trust and dispelling their every fears, these same men, that just before could not stay awake with him for a hour… Well, they must have taken a power nap because they were full of energy. So much so that they eluded, escaped, and out ran their captors, leaving Jesus alone. They must have, *reasonably*, thought that Jesus was quite fit and could take care of himself. Of course.

What happened during the journey from the garden to his midnight rendezvous with the high priest, I'll let you speculate.

When he arrives, he's questioned, mocked, slandered, and struck. (Somebody actually hit the Son of God in the face.) He's brought before the Sanhedrin, and essentially the same thing is done, just with more people this time. Individuals are even brought in solely to lie on him, and the funny thing is, their stories actually contradict each other's. And finally this story begins to take off. The guards and people alike, begin to spit on him. They come up with an idea to verify and validate his divine power. He is blindfolded and struck from every angle, while those who mock and laugh at him implore, "Prophesy. Tell us who hit you!" I would imagine that as he's beaten, bound and blinded, that the pain would cause him to occasionally yell in anguish, letting into his mouth all the spit flying at him at the given moment, along with his own blood. Mind you, this is all supposed to be part of his trial. And I almost forgot. During this trial, Jesus being God, and supernaturally aware, observes one of his closest friends, one he has taken with him everywhere, to witness the most intimate of things, and the one he has chosen to respectfully lead his Church when he returns home, this one, he saw deny ever knowing him. Yet he continues on.

They obviously find him guilty, but since they decided for some reason, to follow this one law, despite all the other laws broken that night, they take him to be tried by Pilate and the Romans. Apparently it's illegal for the Jews to kill during this period of time (Passover).

So he is brought before Pilate, who questions him, amidst the cries of anger and slander, and is found to be innocent of any wrong by Pilate. I must mention that it is now morning, and Christ has had no food, no drink and no sleep. The crowd refuses to accept Pilate's verdict and continue on in the accusation, and I would imagine, their anger is probably elevating through this whole process. Pilate comes upon the information that Jesus is a Galilean, and not knowing what to do about his predicament, sends Jesus on to the jurisdiction of Herod Antipas, the man who cut off his cousin's head, and son of the man who was so intent on killing Jesus as a baby, that he had all the male children, age two or younger in the city of Bethlehem, slaughtered.

When he arrives, beaten, bloodied, bruised, dehydrated, and fatigued from an ordeal that has lasted him through the night, Herod asks for a magic show. Obviously, Herod's request is not accepted, so Herod and his court proceed to mock and degrade Christ, to satisfy their need for amusement, and then merely *dismisses* the Son of God back to the care of Pilate. And still he continues on.

When he's returned to Pilate, Pilate again tries to release him, knowing this man has done no wrong. But as you can guess, the crowd wasn't having it. Pilate even tries to appeal to some form of reason, stating that he will release to them a known, convicted murderer and insurrectionist, or Jesus. Now you must understand that the latter charge of Barabbas [the murderer] was worse concerning the people than the murder part itself, in this time period. See, the Romans did not like civil unrest; not at all. So much so, that they didn't concern themselves with who did what, but anyone found on the street or in the area was suspected of participation and many times killed on the spot, in order to quell the public uproar.

And do you know who the people wanted released? Good ol' Barabbas.

Jesus is now flogged under Pilate's orders. I assume, Pilate hoped that if Jesus was punished, and punishment by the Romans was notoriously severe, this would satisfy the crowds. The instrument used to scourge Christ was not your typical whip though. This was the Roman cat-of-nine tails. Image a whip composed of nine 18-24 inch straps bound together at the handle thereabout. At the end of each strap is an acorn-size piece of lead embedded with shards of glass, nail, and bone fragments. Each stroke rips into the back tearing through flesh and muscle and nerves, revealing the rib bones and fat, with the potential to actually fracture the bones and damage the organs, whether the hit be direct or indirect. As you can image, blood loss would be... I honestly can't find the word. By Jewish law, one cannot be whipped more than 39 repeated lashes, but you see, the Romans had no such law. At some point, the body has to shut down due to the overwhelming pain and blood loss, so many would blackout. Death was not uncommon. Jesus now could see his bones and inwards as his skin and muscles hung from him in countless strips of flesh and tissue. Yet he continued on.

At this point, the series of events according to the different Gospels, show that John saw some things happen in a different order than Mark and Matthew, which potentially could suggest Christ was beaten on two separate occasions, rather than the one most people assume happened at this point. What is for certain is that if Christ *was* just a man, you could say he got the "hell" beaten out of him.

Picture the whole of Pilate's battalion... Somewhere in the upwards of a thousand men strong. Not ten, twenty, thirty. Not a couple hundred, but a thousand men have gathered for the sole purpose of inflicting damage and pain to an already ravaged body. This 'art,' that the Romans had seemed to perfect.

They decided that putting a "crown" comprised of thorns (the date palm has thorns exceeding 12 inches) and a purple raiment of "royalty" would honor "the King of the Jews." They struck him with their hands. They took turns beating him on his head and in his face with a rod, subsequently jamming the thorns in further. They ripped the beard from his face. They spit on him. They blasphemed him. They mocked him as they bowed, yelling, "Hail to the King of the Jews!" Can you imagine the demonic spirits darting back and forth amongst the hundreds releasing all their hate into these tormenters, gloating over the fallen Son of God. I guarantee you, he could see and hear them. Can you see Jesus; not that you would recognize his face? Mary herself wouldn't have been able to. Blood and pus; various other bodily excretions mixed with the oral and nasal fluids of other men streaming down his body. His bones are bruised. Skin and muscle are hanging off in flaps. His inwards exposed to the air. If you looked hard enough, you could probably see his lungs expand as he tries to breath. He had been beaten to the point that he could no longer be recognized as a human.

Now at some point he is brought back out before Pilate and the Jews. Pilate makes a few more attempts to free this man, but the scribes and crowd are not appeased. Jesus must die, and not any old kind of death would do. He had to be crucified. Arguably, the most painful death conceived by men. It's where we get the word "excruciating" from. No compassion could be found. So, Pilate, fearing a riot, or rather what Rome might think of one, concedes to their request. Jesus is handed over to be crucified. And he continues on.

Stripped of the robe as well as his own garments, Jesus is strapped, across his arms and back, to a wooden patibulum, weighing from 80 to 100 pound. Tradition holds that he fell three times on his way to Golgotha. If he had fallen only one time, a forward direction would result in him breaking the 100 lb patibulum's fall with his chin and his chest, and the high probability of a heart contusion. Backwards, and the wood takes his weight dislocating his shoulder, if it's not already out of joint. Either way, the Romans figure out shortly that Jesus was not going to be able to carry it any further. I can't imagine the shape he must have been in for these Romans, who had beaten him to this point, to actually find someone else to carry the cross for him.

They hammer in nails, stroke after stroke, through his wrist, severing his median nerve, causing a severe, perpetual burning sensation. They actually find a nail, rather a stake, that's long enough to go through both feet *and* the wood, not allowing for his legs to move past a bending position. I actually could tell you the lengths of the nails, but image the *size* of three nails that could hold the weight of a grown man. But the Romans were kind enough to tie off his arms to the patibulum for some additional support. As he's raised and hangs there, his "entourage" continues to mock and insult him, apparently having no problem with such a grotesque scene. One that hangs next to him actually has his own share of words. Where he got the energy or audacity to criticize, I would say I don't know, but I do. (We know Satan could not have left such a "marvelous" setting.) Physically now, he has quite the task at hand. As he hangs his weight from his arms, the joints in his upper body are certainly now starting to dislocate, tearing several ligaments and tendons. While the muscles in his chest and ribs stretch, the compression on his lungs allow for no more than a shallow breath. His swollen tongue cleaves to the inside of his mouth adding to his breathing troubles.

He does have an option though. He can alleviate some of the pressure on his chest if he shifts his weight upward. This creates other issues though. His full weight is now on the nail going through his feet, and since he can't lock out his knees, his quads, hamstrings, and calf muscles are sure to knot up and possibly tear. A *conditioned* man cannot sustain a bending position but for so many minutes before his legs give out. So Jesus has the task of going back and forth, position to position, for 6 hours, as his opened back scrapes against this rugged cross.

But all these things together; all of them, are as nothing compared to what he has yet to face.

The One who has never knew sin, in all of eternity past, begins to feel something creeping inside him that he has never felt before. Lust... Greed... Envy... Slander... Rage... Malice... Evil. And then it happens. A weight, unparalleled and immeasurable, crushes him. Every rape, sodomy, molestation, be it victim or predator. Every murder, every drug. Every sorrow, every depression. Every despair, every hopelessness. Every suicide, every cut. Every lie, every curse. Every wicked thought. Every hunger pain. Every fear. Every disease, every viral misery. Every grief, every sleepless night. Every torture, every torment. Every shame. Everything we had become; godless. Every sin, iniquity and affliction, that every man had ever communed with, and ever would, was instantaneously latched to his feeble body.

Through his recognition of every single discrepancy, he notices something far worse. He was alone. His bond to the Spirit and the Father, so fit, that they were One, is now broken. His Father had forsaken him, removing His Spirit and full presence from His only Son. As though he were some kind of wretch. How could this be? He was the pride and delight of His Father. He had never wronged Him, nor disobeyed Him in all of eternity. Reduced to the most pathetic existence, and alone. The King of kings, the Son of the Most High God, and Creator of the worlds was now the lowest of lows. And alone to face Death itself, by himself, and as a man. This was hell. A place void of the communion and presence of an ever-present God.

He has now been formally charged with every crime, issuing *himself* a guilty plea, while at the same time, receiving into himself these same perverse acts themselves, becoming the victim. But this part boggles my mind. Though every sinful act, manifest or not, was placed on him, he did not give in to a single one. Not one. For he was tempted at every point, yet without sin.

I mentioned at the beginning of the chapter that my friend was right about one point, but I never mentioned what that was.

No man could have endured this. It is **flat out** impossible! But Christ was something more, and he *did* do it. I can honestly say I don't know how. We say he accomplished this because of his great love, but this kind of love… the Love it would take to conquer such a literally impossible task, is a love I am fully convinced, no man can *begin* to perceive. But he did it. And though his body should not have been physically capable, he, knowing that his task was complete, proclaimed, "It is finished!" And it was. See Death no longer had power. Death is a by-product of sin. It's merely a "fruit" of sin. He defeated sin. So he went to Sheol (the grave) to accomplish a few things by his legal right, and then told Death to release him. He is risen.

<u>Part II.</u>

¹Who is this coming from Edom, from Bozrah, with his garments stained crimson? Who is this, robed in splendor, striding forward in the greatness of his strength?

"It is I, speaking in righteousness, mighty to save."

²Why are your garments red, like those of one treading the winepress?

³"I have trodden the winepress alone; from the nations no one was with me. I trampled them in my anger and trod them down in my wrath; their blood spattered my garments, and I stained all my clothing.

⁴For the day of vengeance was in my heart, and the year of my redemption has come.

⁵I looked, but there was no one to help, I was appalled that no one gave support; so my own arm worked salvation for me, and my own wrath sustained me. ⁶I trampled the nations in anger; in my wrath I made them drunk and poured their blood on the ground." Isaiah 63:1-6 (NIV)

^{26}*If we deliberately keep on sinning after we have received the knowledge of the truth, no sacrifice for sins is left,* ^{27}*but only a fearful expectation of judgment and of raging fire that will consume the enemies of God.* ^{28}*Anyone who rejected the law of Moses died without mercy on the testimony of two or three witnesses.* ^{29}*How much more severely do you think a man deserves to be punished who has trampled the Son of God under foot, who has treated as an unholy thing the blood of the covenant that sanctified him, and who has insulted the Spirit of grace?* ^{30}*For we know him who said, "It is mine to avenge; I will repay," and again, "The Lord will judge his people."* ^{31}*It is a dreadful thing to fall into the hands of the living God.* Hebrews 10:26-31 (NIV)

I pulled out these two segments to illustrate three points of view. The importance of these viewpoints is that they are valid and true, and legitimized because of the Witnesses themselves.

The first segment is the words of Christ himself, spoken to Isaiah the prophet, concerning His attitude, His mentality in prophetic retrospect of that which would be done to Him.

He doesn't sound very happy at all.

I know we always quote *"For the joy that was set before him, he endured the cross..."* (Heb. 12:2) and that's a great thing to know about our Savior, but we must understand, though we are not permitted to vengeance, to retribution, He is. There will come a day, when Christ will let loose His anger; He will let it go, and what He does, He will do *in* anger. You must understand; He was alone. No one helped Him, at all. **No one**. We say all the time, His love kept Him nailed to the cross, and I believe it did, but He says that what sustained Him through this whole desolate-typed ordeal, was His <u>wrath</u>.

Let me give you the definition of the word "wrath."

Strong, stern, or fierce anger; vengeful anger; deeply resentful indignation; ire (intense

anger). (Random House)

The Hebrew word is defined, "hot, bottles, furious, poison [from the heat]." It also is the Hebrew word for "curdled milk or cheese."

Essentially it can be described as a hot, fierce, rage that festers, becoming bitter and poisonous from the intensity of it. It sours.

The implications are terrifying beyond words. Christ is saying that what sustained Him, what kept Him going in His torment and crucifixion, was the rage of the Almighty, that has been festering, bitterly, from before time began. And this rage is so intense, it has a poisoning affect. He had deep resent, and let no man say otherwise. This does not mean that He did not or does not love the world. That's clear. We have been rectified with no cost, no debt, to ourselves. I bring these things up, though, because He said the day of vengeance is actually in His heart. He thinks about it all the time. The One who died for us, all alone, wants retribution for what was done to Him, and the day is coming where He will have it. Is anyone hearing me? I have to move on.

The second perspective comes from a Father's perspective.

Can you imagine seeing your child go through this, knowing there is nothing you can do?

Has your child been ridiculed? His was.

Has your child been beaten? His was, by hundreds.

Has your child been raped? His was, several times over, including the very same one your own child may have experienced?

Has your child been killed; murdered? Do you see where I'm going with this?

He not only had to sit there and watch; at some point, He has to abandon his little boy, only for the reason that His Son was now guilty of *your* sin. And to put the cherry on top, His Son cries out for Him. *"What have I done, that you would leave me?"* (Mark 15:34) He gives up His Son... for you. How do you think He's going to react, if He places all of sin's consequence on His very own Son, His only kid, for you, and you decide you don't need it? The Bible says you have crucified him "afresh;" (Heb. 6:6) all over again. One time and we get away with it. Not twice...

The third viewpoint, is the Spirit of God. The life-force of God. The Godliness of God. The One who gives grace, unmerited favor; favor that is not earned, nor deserved. He is the Spirit of grace.

You think some lowly "bags of dirt," with some capacity to think, yet wretched in all forms, is going to treat the One who formed and holds together the inner and outer workings of the universe, and everything in it… you think He's going to let these abominations give that kind of treatment to the King, and walk away acting as though nothing happened?

God is just and holy. This is why I have spoken of the need for perfection and justification. For the sake of all parties involved. *"It is a dreadful thing to fall into the hands of the living God."* On that day, there will be no more safety net. There will be no more "what He can do for you." He did his very best. He gave himself. There's nothing more, nothing greater to give. Nothing else. He can have no part in sin. He abandoned His own Son in his time of greatest need in order to separate Himself from sin; so it couldn't touch Him. He despises sin. What do you think He will do to those of us who deserve death?

I was reading in Revelation one day when God began to speak to me concerning the Scriptures.

[10] The same shall drink of the wine of the wrath of God, which is poured out without mixture into the cup of his indignation; and he shall be tormented with fire and brimstone in the presence of the holy angels, and in the presence of the Lamb: [11] And the smoke of their torment ascendeth up for ever and ever: and they have no rest day nor night, who worship the beast and his image, and whosoever receiveth the mark of his name. (14:10-11; KJV)

The smoke of their torment ascendeth up forever and ever...

He then took me back to the Old Testament. There was one thing that appeased Him. One thing that quells His anger when men sinned. Sacrificial purging.

> *[1]And this is the thing that thou shalt do unto them to hallow them, to minister unto me in the priest's office: Take one young bullock, and two rams without blemish*
>
> *[25]And thou shalt burn the whole ram upon the altar: it is a burnt offering unto the LORD: it is a sweet savour, an offering made by fire unto the LORD.*
>
> *[42]This shall be a continual burnt offering throughout your generations at the door of the tabernacle of the congregation before the LORD: where I will meet you, to speak there unto thee.*
>
> Exodus 29:1, 25, 42 KJV

These sacrifices were two-fold in what they represented. Most of us know that when a lamb or ram or dove, etc., was offered up as an offering for sin, that God would see it, and "remember" the sacrifice His Son would pay. But consider the similarities between the descriptions of these two scriptural excerpts.

Sin is an act (thoughts are actions, too) that stems from an evil; an inadequacy that creates an infinite void between our being and His being. God is perfect, flawless; infallible. He is not perfect because He does everything right. He does everything right because He's perfect. Any action that is less than perfect, He literally cannot connect with, even if He wanted to. He is. To grasp that, you have to try to think about a universe without sin. A universe where only He existed. All was good. Then everything that He created was good. No concept of sin. Sin doesn't exist, because its evilness is merely in the fact that it's something God can't do. Therefore He is not capable of empowering one to do so either.

So when we sin, we betray God; we betray everything that is. Sin is not. Essentially it's trash. It's waste. And what do you do with trash, with contaminants? Excessive heat. You burn it. Purified by fire. Even we as Christians, when we stand before the Throne, will be tried by fire. That which is pure, that which is godly will remain. The waste will be burnt up. (1 Corin. 3:13-15) Christ himself has baptized with us with the Holy Spirit and fire. (Luke 3:16) We have been submerged in fire.

Consider also, in God, time is of no consequence. He is eternal. That is *who* He is, that is what He is. There is no beginning for Him, nor end. This is the natural process. This is normal for Him. That is why things that are temporal, including the old heavens and the earth, will be consumed in fire. The opposite of infinite is temporary. Temporary is not a part of Him. So to appease Him, it has to be an eternal appeasing. (You have to try and reason like Him.)

For by one offering he hath perfected for ever them that are sanctified.

Heb. 10:14 KJV

How so? The Bible says *"without the shedding of blood there can be no remission of sin."* (Heb. 9:22) When his blood was shed, it was poured out to cover us [as a means of protection] (1 Corin. 5:7) and cleanse us. (1 John 1:7) The life of any creature is in the blood. (Levit. 17:11,14) Christ as a man, was still God with the Life of God flowing through his veins, and remember, God is eternal. Therefore his blood is never quenched. It never dries up. An eternal sacrifice, for an infinite debt, giving eternal atonement, resulting in eternal appeasement. We who believe, have by faith in the sacrifice (by grace) partook in the sacrifice. The Father can no longer find fault in us.

The only problem is for those that haven't believed. Those that embody sin. There is no other sacrifice to appease a holy and just God. So they themselves become the eternal "sacrifice." A perpetual purging in order that the vengeance and wrath of God, be appeased, and that which can only be eternal. Justice.

Is it unfair, or excessive? Let me say this. He so despises sin, and is so just in His ways, that His own Son was not spared the penalty of sin, though it wasn't even his own. The presence of God was denied to the Son of God.

So let me break this down.

Think on the pain and suffering you have endured in your life. Think about those unbearable days and nights where there seemed to be nothing or no one that could comfort you. Even the people that were present did nothing for you. The pain still isolated you from the rest of the world. Or maybe the world had isolated itself from you. No one cared. No one understood. The times it got so bad, the only thought to comfort you was death.

The times you could start to grasp how a man could take his own life. Think on the worst times, whatever they may be. Understand that even in those times, the presence of God was still with you. He was still there.

You may say, "Well, that says something about His presence." No, it says something about your ignorance; your lack of knowledge, understanding. But there, in the Lake of Fire, there will be no joy. You will not see it. No good thing. Only suffering and pain that cannot be fathomed.

Bill Weise, the author of *"23 Minutes in Hell"*, put it this way: "For those that want to have nothing to do with God, there is a place made just for you." There, the flames are so hot, they will have the capacity to melt every substance in the universe. *But not you.* You know, a supernova has a core temperature of approximately 100 billion Kelvin? That's 180 billion degrees Fahrenheit; 6000 times hotter than the sun.

Peter tells us that on:

"the coming day of God... the flaming heavens will be dissolved, and the [material] elements [of the universe] will flare and melt with fire?" 2 Peter 3:12 (Amplified Bible)

Who could stand under such an affliction..? *You.* You will be given a body "fit for destruction." (Romans 9:22) Not for any period or amount of time. There is no purgatory. We cannot earn salvation now; we certainly will not be able to then. And it will *never* end. Not the slightest bit of relief or mercy.

I say these things for those who have been redeemed as much as I do for those still lost. Child of God, this could have been *your* fate. A godless eternity. I'm not saying that we have to go out and tell everyone we see, every second of every day, that Jesus can save them. Quite frankly, when would you sleep? (I guarantee you Jesus did.) But in truth, how can we continue to just "walk" past multitudes everyday knowing that many to *most* of them are on their way to hell? On their way to this? We have to start doing *something*. Something more than we have been. I could wish this upon no one. We were not made for this. (Matt. 25:41) God Himself knew this to be true. That is why He gave a way out, and it was a Way that cost... so dearly.

Don't know what more to say in this chapter.

The Pissed off Writings of a Prophet

Chapter 8:
Family

What a topic. We want to fix the world, but we don't understand the Church. We want to fix the Church, but we don't even understand the family. I'll try to keep this on some type of track. I guess the best way to go about it is from "top to bottom." I'll try. No promises.

Husband. Dad. Man of God. The one "wearing the pants." The one that leads. The one that "sets the tone." Most importantly, he's the greatest of servants in his domain. This must reflect you, Head of the house. You are called to lead. With respect to authority, there is no equal in your home. So as you go, so goes your house. Yours is truly, the most critical role in the home. I said critical "role." I did not say the most important person or greatest of persons. Your role. Everyone in your house has a role that is crucial to its success, but what is more important, in any unit, than the purpose and direction of the unit? You and you alone are equipped to steer this ship *in the fullness* of God's plan and purpose of those put under your charge. You are no better than anyone in your house. It is even likely that your calling and anointing is not even the most "potent" amongst the members of your family, due to the fact that God is always increasing, even in an immeasurable fashion, and so with each generation He seeks to be glorified more and more... But you, man of God, hold some powerful keys in your hand that are not given to others, nor can they be replicated or reproduced. At least not by anyone but you. (I know a lot of this seems a bit "absolute" but stick with me.)

Woman of God. Wife. Mother. You are truly one of the most powerful forces on earth if not the most powerful (obviously outside of God Himself.) The purpose of your creation was to be a helper to the man. Believe me when I say "helper" is not a little word. In the order of God's creation, you either are, or you are not. You are for God or against Him. As the man was built to lead, you were created and fashioned to help. And though you may not realize it, if you are not acting in the gifting of a help mate, you become a destroyer. Search through the Bible. Amazingly enough, it doesn't spend a lot of time speaking specifically on the principles of being a husband/father or child in a family [relatively speaking], but a woman... The Bible speaks in much greater detail about the ability of the woman in the house to be the blessing that releases the favor of God Himself on the family, or the curse of Death, even to a literal extent. This was not an accident, for several reasons, which I'm just not going to get into right now. You have been fashioned to endure great things with great love and great patience. You have *not* been fashioned to become easily angered, embittered, and a complainer (or a nag). That is not part of your purpose. That's why some of you are so miserable.

Child. Son... daughter... (Man... What *is* your purpose?) Ha-ha... A little joke from a parent's standpoint. Actually from a parent's standpoint, the joke would be that your purpose is to add as much stress as possible to the house. The home is called to be is an environment created for, and conducive to the flourishing of a child in growing and learning concerning the ways of God. In many ways, you can say that the family was made primarily for the benefit of the child.

Unfortunately in today's society, it seems that the child is either used as a legalized "slave" and is not really valued as much more, or the complete opposite; given free reign as the "child-king."

I have to go further into detail with each group, and I would love to start with the man, the head, but I feel quite compelled to actually begin now with the woman, because **Y'ALL HAVE GONE MAD!**

TO THE WOMAN:

Wives, submit yourselves unto your own husbands, as unto the Lord. For the husband is the head of the wife, even as Christ is the head of the church: and he is the saviour of the body. Therefore as the church is subject unto Christ, so let the wives be to their own husbands in every thing. Ephesians 5:22-24 KJV

I don't know how much clearer that can be. Suuuuuuuuu…bmit. As Christ is the **HEAD** of the church… As the church is **SUBJECT** unto Christ…

The Bible says, *"Let this mind be in you which was also in Christ Jesus who being in the form of God, thought it not robbery to be equal with God."* (Philippians 2:5-6)

We have the same mind as Christ and consider ourselves in quality, likeness and substance to be equal with God.

Why?

Because we are one with God.

Why?

Because God Himself has inhabited us, uniting us.

But we do *not* tell God what to do. Do we?

When Christ speaks, we follow.

Why?

Because there is order and hierarchy in a kingdom. Christ submits himself to the will of the Father.

Does that make the Father better than the Son?

No. They are one, of the same consistency.

Submit means to "yield." It's funny, to yield implies I potentially have my own direction, ***BUT*** I will give way to yours. I am going to say something to you, woman, and I really want you to think on this thing. **YOU WERE MADE FOR THIS PURPOSE.** A helper. Help implies assistance. **YOU CAN'T ASSIST YOURSELF.** Do you think you will ever walk in joy and peace outside of the purpose you were created for? And if you have a specific purpose from God, then that means the way He fashioned you reflects that purpose. That's a longer way of saying God has equipped you to complete your purpose. This is the thing with God. He can't get past abundance. So what He's given you will cause to you to *flourish* in the assignment given to you as you *walk* in the assignment given to you.

Well, you don't understand. I've tried that... And my husband is an idiot. Naw, I can't get with that. I'm sorry. I just can't.

My first question to that would be, "Who do you think you are?" Your problem is not really even with your husband. Your problem is with God. You obviously don't trust Him, or have a serious lack of trust. What makes you think you know better than God? When did you get so big, that you can blatantly defy the will of the True and Living God? You're assuming that the commands of God are "conditional," and even more than that, you are the one to decide and determine the conditions. (Here's a couple more side questions: Why did you marry the man in the first place? Did you seek God about it --the marriage-- to begin with?)

Interestingly enough, the Bible does not make qualifications or a requirement that the wife's submission be to a "godly man." I'm saying this in response to those women that feel their husbands are not quite "good" enough for them to follow. Peter tells us (1 Peter 3:1) that the submission of a godly woman has the power to bring salvation (conversion to salvation) to the husband who obeys not the Word. If you carry the power of Life in your submission, the power to bring life from the dead, how much more do you think in your submission, God can bring wisdom to a man you simply consider an "idiot?" And I have to say this; ever consider that maybe you're the "idiot?" I'm not going as far as to say that you're literally an idiot, but maybe you're the one who's lacking wisdom. And maybe... just maybe... he may know what he's talking about. *Regardless*, his conduct does not stop you from moving in a godly fashion.

I really get a kick out of this saying, "If he's a king, then that makes me a queen." **SO WHAT?!** What? You want a title, is that what it is? Women are to be honored by their husbands. (Prov. 31: 28, 1 Peter 3:7) That's Bible. Men should want a woman who is worthy of honor. But honor has never equated to subjection. The word "king" ultimately reflects governing authority. What queen has authority over the king of the KINGdom. Isn't that why they're called "king and queen" and not "the two kings?" (This is just a little reason/logic for you.)

    Consider what a head does for a body. It is the command center. All actions and reaction is controlled there. The body is the facilitator of all the head proposes to do. Consider what problems occur when the body begins to have a mind of its own? How much fear and frustration floods a man (human) when his body begins to do things on its own and he no longer has control of his faculties? What is the damage that can be caused not only to head but the body itself?
Have you ever seen a man with Tourette's syndrome?

In today's age, what I'm inferring in this comparison between the head and the body, and the husband and wife would be considered on the edge of lunacy. At a minimum, quite chauvinistic. But think on this:
    God has made an analogy that has practical application due to its logical comprehensibility. Basically He uses words, objects, and ideas that we logically can make comparisons to without having to fill in the blank for parts we can't intellectually grasp. "Head and body" lead to a relatively simple thought process. What are their functions, and how do they function?
    1 Peter 3:5-6:
        For after this manner in the old time the holy women also, who trusted in God, adorned themselves, being in subjection unto their own husbands: Even as Sara obeyed Abraham, calling him lord: whose daughters ye are, as long as ye do well, and are not afraid with any amazement.

Sarah called her husband "lord," master. "Out of the abundance of the heart, the mouth speaks." (Luke 6:45) She put herself in such a posture of submission that whenever she referred to her husband, she would declare him "One who is supreme in authority." She would affirm his own faith in his ability and responsibility. But notice this, because this is the key. Sarah was one of those "holy women... who trusted God." *I trust **You**, Father. I trust your commandments, your order, and the godly nature you've prescribed to me, more than I do myself and my own desires.* Like her Savior, she "committed [herself] to Him who judges righteously." (1 Peter 2:23) She submitted herself to a means to Life, rather than a means to "self-gratification," understanding her salvation—her joy, her hope, her peace, her freedom, her exaltation, her victory—rested in Christ, in his Way.

Understand something. Your husband, if he be a godly man, is part of the Body of Christ, and as such is not entitled to make decisions of his own any more than you are. Christ is the head of the Body, and even as Scripture specifically says, *"He is the head of the man."* (1 Corin. 11:3) If he be *not* a man who walks in obedience to the Word,

> *Now thanks be unto God, which always causeth us to triumph in Christ, and maketh manifest the savour of his knowledge by us in every place.* 2 Corin. 2:14 (KJV)

Remember your submission in Christ towards him, "without words," can win him.

I must say that I do not, and would not ask my wife to call me "lord." As you take the posture of worship, it is not about you crying "Hallelujah!" wherever you go, but that your life is continually reflecting a fear and reverence for God that keeps you in awe of Him. Keeps you chasing after Him, and pursuing His qualities. Even so, I desire, for godliness and even prosperity sake, that my wife walks in a manner that 'speaks', "In this family, you have supreme authority, because I trust the One who has all authority, and He lives in you."

Funny, I previously used the word "madness" for the "modern" woman. Proverbs 27:17 states,

A quarrelsome wife is like a constant dripping on a rainy day. (NIV)

Proverbs 21:19 instructs,

It is better to live in a desert land than with a quarrelsome and fretful woman. (ESV)

This is Scripture. All Scripture is "God-breathed." (2 Tim. 3:16) That's what your Bible says. Think hard on this. This is not a man's thought on these types of women. This is what God thinks about this kind of woman. This is His "advice." It's pretty amusing as you read over this, but that does not diminish the seriousness of the power a woman holds in her family. As I said, you —wife— can be a bringer of Life and honor to your house, but you can also just as easily bring Death itself.

A wife of noble character is her husband's crown, but a disgraceful wife is like decay in his bones. Proverbs 12:4 (NIV)

Listen, a body cannot live without a head. It will die. I am not claiming you cannot live without a husband over you. Christ is the head of the Body. One body, many members, male or female. But God is unchanging. (Malachi 3:6) He never compromises. His statutes remain forever. (Psalm 119:152) What a man sows, he will reap; God is not mocked. (Gal. 6:7) If you are destroying that man, whether it be intentional or inadvertently, you are destroying yourself. This Scripture says it is like decay in his bones. His bones are part of the constitution of his body. His body equals you. As a matter of fact, the bones make up the frame and foundation of his body. You are destroying your very own foundation in your attempt to establish what you believe to be "independence" and "strength." What I'm saying is that while God deems that man your head, don't "*try*" to submit. God is eternal, and so are all His ways and virtues. If there is an end to it, then it never was in Him to begin. If you "tried" submitting to him then you never started because that which you did, you attempted by your own means, by your own ability. That kind of "submitting" did not originate in God. Live this thing by faith and trust in a God who never fails. He *will* never fail you. Regardless of what appears to happen, never stop, by the life of Christ in you. It is really Christ himself, humbling himself, to the will of Himself, in your husband. One Body, many members. (Romans 12:4)

TO THE MAN:

I had to start with the woman to paint a picture, or at least spark your own picture, of the madness that has defined contemporary relationships seemingly everywhere. Also so that when I say this next statement, you have some context: This is all **your** fault.

Where did this start? It's the "chicken or the egg" question.

- Did the men get tired of leading their family, progressively diminishing themselves and their family to rule of the women?
- Or did the madness creep into women, covertly building and simultaneously tearing down the man, until he had nothing left but resignation or abandonment?

I believe I know the answer but I will not answer it directly, this immediate second. I will start with this. It is *not* your fault that all these women are "crazy." You have no direct control over any man (human). It is not your responsibly to control them. There must be personal accountability in the Kingdom. We will stand before God and answer for every work *we each* have done in this life. We will answer for ourselves and no one else.

What *is* your fault and what you *will* answer for is why you merely sat back and allowed your wife to step outside her role and territory, and "claim" yours. There's more of a problem with that than you know.

Every action is a manifestation of will. The problem there is that, it's never directly your will. You died, but now live in Christ. As I've said before, your every movement and being is the manifestation of the will of Christ (Phil. 2:13), because every wicked thing that you were is gone. But Christ is bound to his own Word and "parameters." He cannot give the rule He's given exclusively to the man, to a woman. SHE IS NOT EQUIPPED. He cannot work through her in that fashion. He has set things in His own order after His own counsel. So my question for your consideration is this:

If her actions are the manifestation of a will not of her own, nor could it possibly be of Christ (he will not move against Himself), what in the hell have you let into your home?

You have sat by and given access to the power of Life and Death [equipped specifically to the woman] over to Satan. And know this, Satan has no interest in Life. (John 10:10)

It is your job, man of God, to never cease in making war with the enemy [even if it is in stillness] in obedience to the Spirit of God, and bring your body, your house, in subjection and submission to the will of God. But pay attention: Scripture declares such things are accomplished *"not by might, nor by power, but by His Spirit."* (Zac. 4:6) If you are the representation of the authority of Christ, you must understand how He worked (and continues to). Christ Himself gives us amazing insight into the manner by which He moves in authority.

[19]Then answered Jesus and said unto them, Verily, verily, I say unto you, The Son can do nothing of himself, but what he seeth the Father do: for what things soever He doeth, these also doeth the Son likewise.

[22]For the Father judgeth no man, but hath committed all judgment unto the Son:

> ^{26}*For as the Father hath life in Himself; so hath he given to the Son to have life in himself;*
>
> ^{27}*And hath given him authority to execute judgment also, because he is the Son of man.*
>
> ^{30}*I can of mine own self do nothing: as I hear, I judge: and my judgment is just; because I seek not mine own will, but the will of the Father which hath sent me.* John 5:19,22,26-27,30 (KJV)

Christ has been given authority to judge-- to rule, govern, determine, resolve, approve, give opinion between right and wrong. He says the Father will not; He's given it to the Son to do. But Christ shows us that despite having been given life and rights to Himself, it still has no means of self-sustainment. He said, "I have been given life in myself, but that life is still tied to a Source; I can do nothing of my own self. Though my Father has delegated to me power to judge --to come to my own conclusions, I will only give place to His. What I see Him do, I do; what I hear Him say, I say." This is how Christ rules, how He leads, how He governs. He trusts Himself to One He knows to be greater. In this, He becomes a servant not only to His Father but moves in His greatest display of love towards His bride. "I have given over my very will and desire. I have given over what I want because my Father's way is True. It is the best. You may not see it. You may not know it. You may even think that I am against you. But I trust Him. He judges righteously. I am not swayed by anything, any circumstance, not even you. I follow Him."

> ^{49}*For I have not spoken of myself; but the Father which sent me, he gave me a commandment, what I should say, and what I should speak.* ^{50}*And I know that his commandment is life everlasting: whatsoever I speak*

therefore, even as the Father said unto me, so I speak. John 12:49-50 (KJV)

    I feel like I am just repeating the same point over and over, but I am trying to get you to see how Christ looks at the order of authority and the process by which He executes it. With this, we see value. Christ says that His commands *are* everlasting life. If we can see value, if we can comprehend it, then we can see the requirement. We will see the necessity.

    Your wife is called to yield herself to her head, which is you. The Bible says she is to do it in the exact same manner that you yourself yield to Christ, being that He is your head. Her ability to do what she is called to, is predicated on the fact that she first has a legitimate example. That's why the Bible uses the word, "as." *As* Christ is the head of the church; *as* the church is subject to Christ. We've established in the Scriptures that she is called to submit to you, as the duty of a wife, but the Bible says that your duty as a husband is not specifically to "rule" or "lead," but the Bible says to "love." To love her as Christ loves you. Believe it or not, this is actually what I've been talking about this whole time.

    I've stated this Scripture before but we have to revisit it. Christ said *"Greater love hath no man than this, that he lay down his life for his friend."* People assume that all He's talking about there is dying for us. The problem is, the Bible says *"if Christ be not risen, then our faith is in vain."* (1 Corin. 15:14, 17) His death shows no love for us if it can do us no good. In His *resurrection*, He has become the Mediator and High Priest for us. (1 Tim. 2:5; Heb. 2:17) So His love was shown toward us not just because He died for us but that He has given his life in service for us.

> ^{42}*But Jesus called them to him, and saith unto them, Ye know that they which are accounted to rule over the Gentiles exercise lordship over them; and their great ones exercise authority upon them.* ^{43}*But so shall it not be among you: but whosoever will be great among you, shall be your minister:* ^{44}*And whosoever of you will be the chiefest, shall be servant of all.* ^{45}*For even the Son of man came not to be ministered unto, but to minister, and to give his life a ransom for many.* Mark 10:42-45 (KJV)

Where people go wrong with this is that they believe when you become a servant you give up authority. That is how it works in the world's system. The Scripture says the "greats" among *us* are to minister, but that does not diminish that which is great, their authority. If we are united as one with God, then no one's greatness can be measured by their substance. Who can be greater than God, and how can He be less than himself? Even so, we've reasoned in the Church, that if the husband loves the woman and "lays his life down" for the woman, that puts her in some position by which she has some variance of authority and equal footing. We will even go as far, without using the words, as to calling the husband into subjection to the woman. But Christ did not set His will aside to the will of those He laid His life down for. He is *their* Savior, and this is His service to them. Their salvation came through His obedience and submission to the will of the Father, who is His Head. (1 Corin. 11:3)

You, husband, are not the Savior, but you, in the manner of Christ, have authority in obedience and submission to the commands of God to bring Life to that which is otherwise dead. If in Christ alone there is Life, then you must give place only to the direction of Christ. That means, regardless of what *she* says or how *she* might treat you, you _do_ only as you hear the Spirit of God speak concerning your situations. **NO ONE ELSE.**

Some would say this is a foolish thing, a foolish saying. Heed no one else? I'm reminded of an event recorded in the thirteenth chapter of 1st Kings. The word of the LORD came to a man of God from Judah, speaking against the altar in Bethel that King Jeroboam of Israel had made (against the LORD's command). The king was using this altar to sacrifice to other gods he had made (against the LORD's command). The man of God spoke prophetically of what would eventually become of the altar and also offered separately a sign that his words were true: the altar would split apart and the ashes on it would be poured out. Jeroboam was angered by this and stretched his hand out in command to seize the man of God. His hand shriveled and subsequently, the sign came to pass; the altar split and the ashes poured out. Jeroboam has a change of heart and asks the man of God to pray for the restoration of his hand. The man of God does and the king's hand is restored. Now we get to the point. Jeroboam offers him food and gifts if he will return with the king. The man of God replies that he would not even take half of everything the king owned, to return and eat and drink with him because God had given this man of Judah specific instruction concerning the matter. He was not to eat bread or drink water and even had to return home by a different route than he took to get there.

The man leaves on a different route back home but at some point stops and is met by an old prophet who lived in Bethel. The prophet beseeches the man to come and eat at his home. But the man of God initially holds fast to the command of the LORD and refuses, citing the instruction he had received from God. The prophet reveals himself as a prophet and tells the man of God he himself has received a word from God. He was to bring back the man of God to his home in Bethel and give him bread and water. The problem was the Bible tells us the prophet was lying. Unfortunately the man of God concedes to the request of the prophet and returns to the prophet's house to dine.

Now I am persuaded that this old prophet was truly a man called by God, predominately for two reasons. One, the Bible identifies the man as an "old prophet." God has never had trouble distinguishing prophets from "false prophets." And two, the word of the LORD condemning the man of God for his disobedience came through the old prophet himself. The man of God had ate bread and drank water in the place God had commanded him not to and so he would not be buried in the tomb of his fathers. He was on his way home when he was killed by a lion. Now this part is rather interesting. The lion and the donkey simply waited by the body. When do lions kill and not eat? What kind of donkey does not flee in terror? The questions could keep going, but this was an obvious set-up. Hear me, God Himself will try you on His Word. This was a true man of God that clearly demonstrated the power of God in obedience but because he decided to listen to another man instead of *all* God had told him to, there was a price to pay. And to think! The man he listened to was a genuine prophet [who would later show great care for his remains and even *confirmed* the word of the LORD the man of God spoke to the king]. One of my favorite personal sayings is "Mess around with God…" You can try God if you want to. He will win every time! We must hold fast to what God speaks by His Spirit to us, even personally. Especially personally. Regardless of who would say or do otherwise.

Well see, that just ain't right. You need to pay attention to your wife, cause she's supposed to help you. God

speaks to her too. The husband ain't the only one God speaks to. Just like Sarah. She told Abraham to get rid of the slave girl and her son. And what did Abraham do. He listened to his wife, and he did it.

(Wow... It's been awhile since I've heard from you.) You are correct... about a few things. The husband should give place to his wife considering especially that she *is* a child of God, the Spirit of God *does* speak to her, and she *is* anointed to **ASSIST** him. But consider this: Sarah *was* speaking the truth, but Abraham, called the father of faith, did not move **until** the Spirit of God spoke to him personally and confirmed the Word of God in her. There is nothing at all wrong with paying attention to what your wife would say to you. She may know something you don't. *"Two are better than one."* (Eccles. 4:9) But as Christ has spoken concerning himself as the template of a husband to his bride, "I *only... only* do what my Father does. I *only* say what my Father says." As I just spoke on before, consider if any man were to tell you what to do, and you merely took him at his word. What happens when you stand before God and He asks you why you did what you did? What are you going to say? "Because he told me to..?" Or, "Because my wife told me to. Man, you don't know her. She is a witch, she is a terror..." Have you not exalted the word of man (humans) above the Word of God? Have you not also placed your own "comfort" and what you consider to be "self-preservation and peace" of greater value than that which God offers us in Himself? You are moving by fear, which is the antithesis of faith. You are actually moving in fear towards your *wife*.

The issue is that this is all a distraction. *"We wrestle not against flesh and blood..."* (Eph. 6:12) Her "scorn" is a perversion of her emotions. It is an atmosphere conducive for Satan. But let's actually take a step back before we go further.

We know that men and women psychologically operate from two different stand points. Men tend to operate from a rational and logical approach to life. Women are emotional creatures. Men tend to be calculating and fundamental. Women tend to be very experiential and impulsive. Men have singular focuses; one thing at a time. Women have much broader focuses; how much can I take in at once, how much can I do at once? Men are introspective; "Let me figure this out." Women tend to live outwardly; "Girl... what do you think?" Am I getting anywhere with this? Are you seeing some fundamental differences? We as humans will definitely mix and match with variances of these traits. But that which was "feminine" about the man was taken from the man in the beginning, and a woman was made. But the man was left with everything he would need to complete the role God had established for him before He even created man. *"Let us make man in our image and after our likeness..."* (Genesis 1:26) So He had given name to us before the manifestation was brought to pass. He had given identity and definition that reflected Himself and even within Himself is hierarchy. And so, that is the question? Who will lead? Men and women have distinguishing qualities and in all of them you can find value; great value. They are the qualities of God Himself. But they no longer exist in one, they have been divided. Who will lead? Who can lead? Who would *you* want to lead? Which one would *you* chose? What traits would you give the one who would have authority over you; the one that would hold your life in the balance? Would you want someone who thinks rationally or one who goes as their emotions go? Someone who calculates their situation or one that is moved impulsively by the experience of a situation? One that moves one step at a time, or one that tries to take the whole thing at once? Would you have a leader who can self-reason, or one that needs the opinions of everyone else? On general principle, one sounds like the best of leaders, and the other sounds like the worst.

So this is the issue. As I said before, there are definitely variances in the measure of traits and characteristics that define humans, as much as each human is different individually. But that does not negate that these traits are present and prevalent. You have what you've been given, and so are gifted. Your wife has also been gifted. Each gift, though, has a specific design and purpose. What happens when you encounter a situation you are not equipped for? So many will use what they *do* have. The problem is what you have is not made for that, so you will try to "stretch" the thing you are using. You pervert its original purpose. If you try to use a screw driver to hammer in a nail, best-case, you waste some time; worst, you harm yourself and damage the screw driver.

Your wife has only what God has given her, the same as you. We can create no more. So if she or anyone else tries to extend her, she is moved into the area of perversion. This is the atmosphere conducive to the Enemy. He himself is no creator, but has become fatally effective at using the gifts of men as weapons against them. And your wife is an emotional creature gifted to use her emotions in her pursuit of edifying her family. (Please understand that I'm not trying to define a woman as a ball of emotion. I'm using that which is a major part of what defines her process.)

I stated I would not directly answer the "chicken/egg" question until the appropriate time had come. And so it hath now cometh uponeth-eth us...

So what came first?

Did the men get tired of leading their family, progressively diminishing themselves and their family to rule of the women?

Or did the madness creep into women, covertly building and simultaneously tearing down the man, until he had nothing left but resignation or abandonment?

And the answer is... neither, because it was a variance of both [which actually makes the question somewhat irrelevant, but I will explain this]. This thing has a cyclical nature. Let me add this too, the spirit realm works like a vacuum, and by the nature of a vacuum, as something is vacated, something else fills in. The man is fatigued and so "gives" some "executive" powers to the wife. But God is not in it, so Satan fills in bringing a rebellious and maddening spirit. And so/Or... the wife begins to think more of herself and her ways than the order of God and commences to rise against her husband, and so his bones, his foundation, begins to weaken causing him fatigue. Any number of variation in these scenarios can be the cause, but regardless, they begin to feed on one another, as *both* happen. The man gets more and more fatigued, diminishing away, and the woman becomes more and more "independent" and rebellious. But this is what makes the question ultimately irrelevant. Though the woman can fall back in righteousness and submit, she cannot lead, and she cannot make you. Though her submission gives place for you to lead it has no direct means of establishing you in action. You, however, walking in your authority, directly establish order by virtue of authority and the One that has given it. You, walking in godliness will cause her to walk in submission, or there is no victory in Christ. I will put no time-table on it, but two cannot contend forever. The Bible tell us that *"two cannot walk together unless they're in agreement."* (Amos 3:3) Someone has to give and so someone will give. But the Bible tells us something else, *"Resist the devil and he will flee."* (James 4:7) This is your enemy. This is the enemy of your wife. Your wrestle is not with your wife. She is your beloved and the Word says *"the weaker vessel."* (1 Peter 3:7) See her as Christ sees you. See her as Christ sees *her*. Protect her. Care for her. Show compassion towards her. Lead her. Love her [unconditionally]. *"The love of **God** is shed abroad in your heart."* (Romans 5:5) No one can do this for you. You can't even do this for yourself. Your familial ministry, your service, your duty, your love is service unto your wife, by your obedience and submission to God, and God alone.

TO THE CHILD:

It seems sometimes that you are put in the worst position. You do not choose your family. You can't get out. Even if you could, where would you go? You have minimal say in the direction the family will take, and so consequently you have relatively little influence in the initial directing of your *own* life. I do not say this to say you should have more; there's a reason you are the child and they are the parent(s). But, it does not change the fact that there's no step-by-step manual for parenting, and the same people that made all those completely stupid decisions and mistakes, are now *your* parents. They can't seem to hold their own lives together, but they can tell you how to? You're smarter than they are, right? Maybe so. Maybe so...

I will say this to you. *"There is nothing new under the sun."* (Eccles. 1:9) Circumstances and situations vary, but the principles and precepts remain unchanging. Everything that happens has happened before. By virtue of living, your parent(s) have learned things. There are things that remain constant in men due to the fact that they are human, and even how they interact with their environment. Certain things have been set in order by

God Himself, and though your parent(s) may or may not know God, they have spent a lifetime learning whether their actions move with or against the order of God, and what the consequences are. When you were a "youngling", your parent(s) would have to take precautions to make sure you didn't "cook" your hand on a stove, because you had no concept of the action and consequence. You may be older now and have learned some great fundamentals in life, but the process has not stopped for your parent(s) either. They have also grown and learned. Even from the stupid mistakes you saw them make.

I would imagine that most kids, as they get older, begin to see their parents as "idiots." I wish I could tell you that that's not true. *"As you get older, you'll begin to understand why they..."* and all that stuff. All that jazz. I would be a fool to say that *all* adults are idiots, but truly, the older I get personally, the dumber the things I see people do. The less I see that people have a grasp of what's going on. Even people that undeniably would be attributed as intelligent. And so I've come to realize that people are not "idiots" merely because they have less aptitude than someone else. (That someone else will have less than another.) People act in a mind of stupor because they don't have wisdom; godly revelation. And so their worldview, their foundational knowledge is skewed or distorted, leaving essentially nothing but distorted conclusions. I say all this to tell you—child— get wisdom. God tells you to honor and obey your parents. (Eph. 6:1-2) It is a principle and the Bible actually says that it comes with promise from the One who works everything for your good. As it is with a wife who is called to submit to her husband, God is not a fool. He is not short-sighted. He understood that circumstances may not look as you would desire them to, but He, in His love, has worked out and set in order everything after the counsel of His own will. His promise for you is Life and hope. He is not trying to destroy you and He is not against you, though your circumstance may seem to be. As I said, circumstance may vary. But faith is still required for all men, young or old.

I tell you the truth. As God speaks very specifically about the functioning of a wife, He speaks in great detail about His care for the child. God has always been One to take special notice of those not in position to stand up for themselves; those that seem to be open for exploitation. And He takes that offense very seriously.

> *⁵"Whoever receives one such child in my name receives me,*
>
> *⁶but whoever causes one of these little ones who believe in me to sin, it would be better for him to have a great millstone fastened around his neck and to be drowned in the depth of the sea."*
>
> *¹¹"See that you do not despise one of these little ones. For I tell you that in heaven their angels always see the face of my Father who is in heaven."* Matt. 18:5-6, 11 (ESV)

He takes special interest in your well being. But this does not equate to your "idea" of a perfect scenario. In this life, people are going to wrong you. Those same people may happen to be your parent(s). On the flip side, your parent(s) may actually have not wronged you at all, but you feel they have. These things become irrelevant, when it concerns your obedience and honor first and foremost to God and subsequently his commands. I have learned a great deal from both my parents, but many times what stands out to me is what I learned **not** to do as a parent and person. I say this to say a couple things.

One, you can learn and increase from everything, at least while you remain on this earth (There is nothing else for you to gain, if you were to perish into a godless eternity). No one else needs suffer from you what you have suffered from your parent(s). The Bible says that in our affliction we learn the statutes of God. (Psalm 119:71) You've seen your parent(s) failings and what it has cost them; even what it cost you. Be better. This is the true desire and motivation of any parent that loves their child.

Two, the failings of my parents do stand out to me, but the goodness of the life that I live, comes from many of the attributes and teachings instilled in me by them, that have seemingly gone unnoticed. It was in their attempts to care for me, that I learned self value and a model of care for others. They didn't *try* to do some things bad and some things good. They simply lived. They used what they knew, and in the process and relationship, I gleaned goodness wherever it was found creating in so many ways the man I am today.

This is another thing God is not short-sighted about. You cannot be short-sighted about a circumstance you created in the midst of a story you created; a universe that is fashioned and moved by your will and desire.

> [26]*And He made from one [common origin, one source, one blood] all nations of men to settle on the face of the earth, having definitely determined [their] allotted periods of time and the fixed boundaries of their habitation (their settlements, lands, and abodes),* [27]*So that they should seek God, in the hope that they might feel*

after Him and find Him, although He is not far from each one of us. Acts 17:26-27 (Amplified Bible)

God established you; the span of your life, the location it would take place, even the lineage that you would come from, so that it would cause you to seek Him. Your parents are your parents by no happenstance or coincidence. Good, bad, and/or ugly, they are who they are and the way they are for a reason. Put your hope in God. Your parents don't have to be godly for you to be. Everything God has established as good dies before it reaches the fruition of life, including Himself. Give your life over to God. Humble yourself. Honor and submit yourself to those who have rule over you. (Heb. 13:17) You will be exalted by God Himself. There is nothing more, nothing greater, nothing better than that. Be patient. There is a grace given for each task. One thing you will never be again is a child on this earth. Gain all you can gain while this specific form of favor rest on you. You will not always be a child, but you are never too young to serve God. John the Baptist was filled with the Spirit of God from birth. (Luke 1:15) You have been given opportunity to store up treasures in heaven that will never present itself again by virtue that we will only live one life and this life has an expiration date. So do right by God. He has already done right by you. I leave you, young one, with words that have produced great confidence and purpose for me in my own youth.

Let no one despise or think less of you because of your youth, but be an example (pattern) for the believers in speech, in conduct, in love, in faith, and in purity.
1 Timothy 4:12 (Amplified Bible)

The Pissed off Writings of a Prophet

Chapter 9:
Final Thoughts

Congratulations! You've made it through the book. I'm actually surprised, at least to some extent. I've recounted to you everything He's told me to. I've studied the Scriptures for years, as so many others have, but I've come to see that while people continue to search out and chase the wisdom of God, even through the Scriptures, they go into their studies with preconceived notions. Their premises have already been established outside the Word and so their conclusions from reading the Word lead to concepts that have no Biblical foundation, but we call it "God." The precepts, the "original" commands, the "before" commands, are not accurate to what our preceding God has laid out and so we cannot help but come to skewed conclusions. Though we love to believe it, we do not go into the Bible looking for a foundation, because tradition and "life experience" has already taken that place; we have no "need" any more for one. Since life experience changes and the foundation of tradition can easily be lost, theology shifts and evolves over time, and so the Bible becomes an addition rather than the standard. But our faith dictates it must be the standard, so we've conformed, and essentially perverted the statutes of God to mean something different than what is even said, and cannot figure out why His Word seems so conditional. We cannot figure out why sometimes we get "lucky" and it seems to work, but more often than not, nothing happens. Nothing that we really believed for; not really the thing we were believing to happen.

    I had a dispute with my mother when I was about twelve years old. She told me it was about that time that I started to get into the Bible for myself. I needed to begin reading and studying and renewing myself in the Word on a daily basis. I was of age now where I could understand for myself what I was reading and this was the godly thing to do. While I agreed what she was saying was valid, I didn't believe it applied to me. I had grown up in the church. I'm a very intelligent individual. I have a great memory. I knew all the stories. I had a pretty good base of a lot of the "marquee" Scriptures. Knew the catch phrases. Basically I already knew the Bible. *"I'm young and I have a lot of time to learn as I go. Besides I love God, I'm saved, I follow Him (as best as I know how), and what I know is obviously enough. Heck, I'm saved!"* And I was saved, but the problem was that essentially everything I knew about God was others' thoughts, others' theology. So every conclusion I would come to would be dictated by a flawed perception of life stemming from my own limited life experience (limited by virtue, in that it's temporal) and the traditions of men, good or bad. As I said, tradition can quickly become vain because the [foundational] reasoning for doing them many times is forgotten or ignored.

    Over the next few years I would read my Bible in spurts but nothing that would constitute a yielding or devotion to the pursuit, and interestingly enough my spiritual life significantly began to suffer during this period. (That story's for another day.) At 16 though, everything changed. To keep this short, basically God forced His hand and said, "You've wasted enough time." I began to study the Scriptures hours at a time, day after day after day. As I studied, I definitely recognized many things I had been taught, but I was also coming across principles that were making no sense with the foundations that had been planted in me. So this drove me deeper and deeper in my searching and reading. Eventually I would see more and more things that would line up with the principles I had come across, and this now was breaking apart and tearing down so much that I had been taught, not only "locally" but what I was hearing everywhere. I began to see people were completely misunderstanding these "marquee" Scriptures because their context for them was rooted in what they had been taught themselves, rather than the reality of what the Scriptures were actually saying. To put it frankly, I was at the point of, "Father, what the hell are they talking about?" (And sadly, so many times, I'm still there.)

All that said is a whole lot to get to this point. Actually, I really wrote this book to get you to this point. Read the Word for yourself. Study the Scriptures for yourself. Seek out God for yourself. I tell everyone I come across in this context, do not simply take my word for this. You have a personal relationship with God for a reason. God does not want to be found of the masses or the collective. He wants to be found of you. To put it another way, He doesn't want to be a friend of a friend. All my wisdom, all my revelation will be accounted to me. (Not to say that those that have contributed will not be credited as well.) We cannot live off each other's faith. You have to grasp the things of God for yourself. This is the reason why we can preach the gospel until we're "blue in the face" and it will seemingly have zero impact. We can break it down as simple as our minds can possibly get and still be on different worlds with our audience. (Believe me, this can be a daily occurrence for me.) But for the sake of His own glory, God gives revelation. I can teach every precept I know, but God birthed it in me personally. Therefore, I know how I got here and so I know how it applies to me. No one but you and God have real understanding of everything your life has become, so you must search out this personal Jesus, personally for personal wisdom and personal application. No one can do this for you, and this is the reason why we as a Body are **FAILING**. Everyone wants to push their particular brand of Jesus *universally*, and if they're not pushing their own, they're looking for someone else's to leech off. We push for unity, but we call for unity to be dictated by the biggest name of a man we can "see." We're like Israel searching for a king (1 Samuel 8), instead of letting Christ be King. Consider the Bible actually says that you need that no man should teach you because of the anointing of God. (1 John 2:27) Because of the Spirit that leads and guides into all truth. (John 16:13) Many would refute that. Many *godly* people would refute that, citing that this is what leaders [in the Church] are for. Understand there's a difference between what is deemed necessary and what can still be used. If God does not use men to edify and build one another, then there is no point for this book. But the Bible gives us a foundation to build on, not to ignore. The Spirit of Truth has granted such access to us that He would clearly state, "You need no one to inform you but Me." This empowers us. It builds us. It brings a confidence and assurance that we serve a God that not only can be reached but desires to reach back. The notion that you ***need*** a "leader" to teach you implies, that though it is the Spirit of God speaking and teaching, He needs to go through one man to get to another man. Unless, you're implying that what is being said does not come from the Spirit, and you have your own thoughts to contribute that are just as vital to building up of another.

> *For there is one God, and one mediator between God and men, the man Christ Jesus.* (1 Timothy 2:5)

Jesus said that His sheep know His voice. (John 10:4) You don't have to be "five-fold," "leader," "ministry worker," or simply just validated by men. *"My sheep..."* Sheep. That's his promise to you. *"A stranger they will not follow."* (John 10:5) Promise.

From the greatest to the least of us, the Body of Christ has to get a hold of this. We have a God who simply wants to be God. He's given up everything for it. He's laid out everything He's seen fit to, which is also everything that is needed to be like Him. Now He's simply looking for a people who will give up everything for Him. The problem is everyone thinks this is about what is merely [and truly] the outward. The money, fame, friends, family, comforts, reputation, time, etc. These are small things. What is money to a God who walks on gold? What is fame and reputation to a God so "big," His glory is visible? What are friends and family to a God who makes men from dust? What is comfort to a God that considered it joyous to endure a cross? What is time to a God that has no beginning or end? These are very small things to Him. He doesn't need to take yours.

He wants your soul, your "mind." This is the "everything" He wants from you. This is what He wants for Himself. He wants you to think like He thinks. To see like He sees. To move like He moves. To do what He does when He does. He wants an extension of Himself that has His capability to see in the fullness how great He is. How awesome and amazing and terrible and dreadful He is. He wants those that can recognize the Truth, and from that recognition, to simply live It. And He has understood, He is the only one capable of making this so.

This is all I have left for you now:

²⁸And it will be that as I have watched over them to pluck up and to break down, and to overthrow, destroy, and afflict [with evil], so will I watch over them to build and to plant [with good], says the Lord. ²⁹In those days they shall say no more, The fathers have eaten sour grapes, and the children's teeth are set on edge. ³⁰But everyone shall die for his own iniquity [only]; every man who eats sour grapes--his [own] teeth shall be set on edge. ³¹Behold, the days are coming, says the Lord, when I will make a new covenant with the house of Israel and with the house of Judah, ³²Not according to the covenant which I made with their fathers in the day when I took them by the hand to bring them out of the land of Egypt, My covenant which they broke, although I was their Husband, says the Lord. ³³But this is the covenant which I will make with the house of Israel: After those days, says the Lord, I will put My law within them, and on their hearts will I write it; and I will be their God, and they will be My people. ³⁴And they will no more teach each man his neighbor and each man his brother, saying, Know the Lord, for they will all know Me, from the least of them to the greatest, says the Lord. For I will forgive their iniquity, and I will remember their sin no more. Jeremiah 31:28-34 (Ampified Bible)

This day has come, 2000 years ago.

Symeon Cabell

Biography of Symeon Cabell

Symeon Cabelll is a prophet, called form birth, but made aware of his gifting at the age of 16. At the young age of 3, he professed Christ as his Savior and has been preaching the Gospel since. He has served as a youth pastor, team (collegiate football) chapel minister, and co-leader of a collegiate Athletes in Action chapter. He also attended North Dakota State University on a football scholarship and currently works as a graphic designer. He and his wife, Shyla, have three children, daughter Sivan, and two sons, Samari and Shammah.

Symeon Cabell

the pissed off writings of a prophet

www.ingramcontent.com/pod-product-compliance
Lightning Source LLC
Chambersburg PA
CBHW051444290426
44109CB00016B/1673